Choosing the Players

GW00598876

Penny Hackett is Company Training and Development Manager at Clarks International, based in Somerset. She was formerly Course Director for personnel management courses at Kingston Business School and a member of the Institute of Personnel Management National Education Committee.

Educated at St Anne's College Oxford and Kingston Polytechnic, she has experience of personnel and training in organisations spanning the service and manufacturing, public and private sectors. She has been involved in a wide range of consultancy activities and carried out research into how newly qualified personnel practitioners get jobs.

She has written a number of books and articles, including *Success in Management: Personnel, Interview Skills Training: Practice Packs for Trainers* and *Personnel: The Department at Work* (IPM, 1991).

Other titles in this series

Keeping the Team in Shape by John McManus
Getting a Result by Iain Maitland

We are grateful to the National Federation of Self Employed and Small Businesses Ltd for their help and cooperation in the preparation of this series.

The Institute of Personnel and Development is the leading publisher of books and reports for personnel and training professionals and students and for all those concerned with the effective management and development of people at work. For full details of all our titles please telephone the Publishing Department on 081 946 9100.

Managing People in the Small and Growing Business

Choosing the Players

Penny Hackett

Cartoons by Katherine Bowry

Institute of Personnel and Development

Typesetting by The Comp-Room, Aylesbury
and printed in Great Britain by
the Cromwell Press, Wiltshire

British Library Cataloguing-in-Publication Data
A catalogue record for this book is available from the
British Library

The views expressed in this book are the author's own and may not necessarily reflect those of the IPD.

**INSTITUTE OF PERSONNEL
AND DEVELOPMENT**

IPD House, Camp Road, London SW19 4UX
Tel: 081 946 9100   Fax: 081 947 2570
Registered office as above. Registered Charity No. 1038333
A company limited by guarantee. Registered in England No. 2931892

Contents

1 Defining the Game

 Whatever business you are in, your company must have its own special product or service proposition. If you are not able to satisfy the wants of your present and future customers more quickly, and/or less expensively, and/or to a higher standard than your competitors, you will not be in business for long. Your manufacturing or service *operations* are at the core of your business.

Simply being able to do these things is not enough. Unless enough people know you can, and are willing to buy what you have to sell at a price which enables you to keep on making a profit, you will soon become a business failure statistic. Effective *marketing* of your business proposition is therefore essential.

And unless your business has a firm financial base, sound positive cash flow and prudent financial management, once again you will fail. So careful *accounting* is imperative.

All three of these business functions – accounting, marketing and operations – are vital for success. None of them can be done effectively unless you have:

1

- the right people
- doing the right things
- in the right way
- at the right time
- in the right place
- at the right price

continuously to exceed your customers' expectations. Even in the smallest business, the effective management of *people* is therefore the real key to business success – which is, after all, the name of the game.

Just like a sports team or the cast of a play, each member has their own talents. Bring them together in a way that enables each to make their own best contribution to a clear team objective – and you have a winning combination. Fail to make use of their individual abilities, force them to work in ignorance of the real objective or of what they can do to help achieve it, and you have a recipe for a performance which, at most, falls well short of being the best you can be.

As soon as your business becomes more than a 'one-person band', you will start to think about getting the right team together. In later chapters, we will explore some of the ways in which you can organise the work and find the best people to do it. Here our focus is on exploring the pros and cons of building a stable team of employees.

Of course, you may have decided that you do not wish to get involved in the complexities of actually taking people onto your payroll. Instead you may choose to sub-contract work to other firms or self-employed individuals. We will explore this, and a range of other options, in Chapter 2.

Continuity versus regular 'substitution'

One of your options as a potential employer is never to employ anyone for more than two years. If you treat all your employees as temporary, whether or not you agree this with them and formally create a short-term contract, you can avoid many (though not all) of the legal obligations which arise once people have been on your payroll for more than two years.

At first sight this seems attractive. It means, among other things, that you can:

- part with people without a redundancy payment should you no longer need them
- sack someone whose conduct, work standards or attendance record don't come up to scratch, without having to pay compensation and (provided there is no question of discrimination) without the fear of being taken to an industrial tribunal – though you should always observe any relevant formalities, such as notice requirements
- regularly review exactly what work needs to be done and what skills are needed to do it, recruiting new people with the right talent rather than incurring the expense of retraining the old ones
- frequently bring in people with new ideas and ways of working, to challenge some of the assumptions you take for granted. This can be very healthy for a business. Without some stimulus from outside it is all too easy to stagnate.

The downside of such flexibility can be instability. If your team is made up of too many people who have no long-term stake in the success of the business, you will need to consider much more carefully how to get the best from each in the short term. And if you think you can get the best of both worlds by hiring the same person on a series of short-term contracts – think again. In certain circumstances such contracts count towards continuity of employment and so give the employee the very redundancy and unfair dismissal rights you are trying to avoid.

Remember, too, that regardless of their length of service, every person who leaves your business takes away:

- the skills you have helped them develop
- the knowledge of your business and business processes they have acquired
- the contacts they have made while working for you.

All of which may now be put to use for one of your competitors. Departing employees can also take away:

- odd bits of equipment, uniform, stationery and so on, which it may not be worth trying to reclaim but which *could* be used to your detriment and do represent a cost to the company
- the intangible contributions they have made to helping your business to function. It may not be part of anyone's formal job description, but lose the person who organises the company's social events, or the one who knows how to take the tension out of difficult meetings with some well-timed humour – and you will miss them.

And every new person who arrives must:

- learn to apply their skills and knowledge in a new context, quite possibly with a boss and colleagues whose expectations of them differ from those of their previous employer
- get to know their way around your business, its people, terminology, systems and methods of working
- win acceptance from their colleagues and customers.

Some will also need to acquire new knowledge and skills. Even if they don't, and even if you have selected someone with real ability, they are unlikely to work at their full potential for the first few days, weeks or even months, as they settle in and find their feet.

Selecting new people to work with is not easy, and there is always the risk that you will pick someone who *isn't* right for your business. If you regularly recruit people on short-term contracts, the chances are you won't always get it right. If you get it wrong, and choose someone who hasn't got what it takes, then you will face other problems.

For a start, you will have wasted time and money on fruitless recruitment and perhaps training. You will have had days, weeks or months of sub-standard performance. This can be a double loss: you will have sacrificed necessary output, paying wages for little or no return; and the ill-chosen recruit may actually have antagonised customers, suppliers or colleagues through their incompetence. This will reflect badly on the business as a whole.

If you act too quickly to remedy the mistake by sacking the offender, other employees may think you are being hasty or unfair. If you don't act quickly enough, they may resent having to carry a passenger. Whenever you act, there will be the stress, for you and the employee, of parting. Usually this will just be the sleepless night before you bite the bullet. Occasionally your ex-employee may create real difficulties for you – perhaps by alleging they have been dismissed on the grounds of pregnancy, race, sex, or trade union activity. Dismissal for any of these reasons is illegal from day one of employment.

For all these reasons, it makes sense to try to create a measure of confidence and stability in your team.

When you come to weigh up the pros and cons of stability versus flexibility for *your* business, you may find you get more than one answer. There may be some areas in which stability will be beneficial – perhaps because of the complexity of the work involved or the need to build and maintain customer relations. In others, flexibility and new ideas may be vital to keep ahead of the competition.

Much will depend on the nature of the roles to be filled, which in turn depends on what your business does and how it is organised. So before we start to look in detail at the process of recruitment itself, we will pause to consider some of the different ways in which the key roles in your team may be allocated.

Planning the team

Many small businesses develop around the skills and entrepreneurial instincts of just one or two people. Many of our largest corporations started that way, too. At some point in their history, the founders recognised the need for help – for people with whom the work could be shared – to enable the business to grow.

Sometimes it is easy to see what you need. If the skills of the founder are all to do with technological innovation and product creation, he or she may readily recognise that it makes sense to concentrate on that, and to bring in someone else to go out and market the product, keep the books and manage the people. If the founder's skills and interests are less specific, the answer may be less obvious.

How you approach the solution will depend on where you stand at present. If you already have a number of specialists working for you, and/or if you have set up particular individuals or groups with a specific focus, you probably won't want to go back to square one and rethink. If, on the other hand, everyone you currently employ is a Jack (or Jill) of all trades, working at the same level on the same assortment of tasks, you might find the following questions provide a useful framework for beginning to think about how best to divide up the work of your company.

What are you in business for?

For most people, the answer will include something to do with making money, for themselves and any other shareholders. For some, the emphasis will be very much short term – to make a quick killing and retire to the South of France. For others, it will include building a firm financial base to be passed on from one generation to the next.

For most, making money is probably not the *whole* answer. Becoming the best, being the first choice for customers, being at the leading edge of development in the industry, helping to make the world a safer, healthier or more exciting place, providing interest, employment or a sense of purpose for those involved, or just wanting to be your own boss – all these may be part of your company's reason for being.

Whatever the answer, it will have a major bearing on the way you choose to do business and, in particular, on the way you treat your customers, suppliers and employees. If you are in business for the long term, and want to get and keep loyal customers, you will need to plan your work in a way that best serves *their* needs, rather than what is administratively convenient for you.

What are the key *functions* that must be carried out within your business?

This is not the same as asking what jobs there are. As we have seen, in all businesses there are operational functions – to do with designing and delivering goods or services. In a retail business, these functions will be concerned with buying stock for resale, merhandising the shop and serving customers. In a manufacturing or processing one, they will revolve around the design and development of the product, the purchase of raw materials and transforming them into the finished item, packing and perhaps transporting them. In a hotel, the purchase of food and other supplies, and the provision of housekeeping and catering services would fall into this category.

To support these operations, a number of other functions are necessary. Activities to draw your products and services to the attention of potential customers and to persuade them to buy can be drawn together under the general heading of sales and marketing. Work to ensure that invoices are sent to customers, payment collected and banked, accounts kept, taxes and employees paid is part of the accounting function. Among the other functions which may be needed are those to do with renting, heating, lighting, furnishing and maintaining your business premises, those to do with getting and keeping staff, and those to do with ensuring that the company fulfils its legal obligations.

Each of these functions requires some degree of record keeping and monitoring to enable results to be measured and improved. This in turn *may* mean that there are computer systems design, programming, data collection and reporting functions to be carried out.

Depending on the size and complexity of the company, you may decide to split these functions so that each is handled by a different person. The basis upon which you decide to group them together will tend to be the knowledge and skills of the people currently working in the business, rather than any more abstract analysis. Nevertheless, it will pay to look at the options through the eyes of your customers as well as those of your employees. If your customers find themselves unable to follow the logic of who does what when dealing with you, it may be time for a rethink.

What are the key *processes*?

Your customers are not interested in the functions being carried out inside your business. Their only concern is the output which results from your activities. In particular, they either want and

8

are prepared to pay for the goods and services you produce, or they are not. So how do you bind all the separate functions together to make sure your customers get what they want?

The answer is to think in terms of *processes*. Whatever other aims and objectives you may have, in reality your business is about transforming inputs into outputs. The inputs may include ideas, knowledge, skill, cash and physical materials. The outputs can be anything from a comfortable night's sleep (if you run a guest house), to a carrier bag full of groceries (if you run a shop), to an attractive and secure home (if you are a house builder).

The processes through which you convert inputs into outputs are the thread running through your business. They are the channels along which information, materials and other resources flow. If they are well designed and functioning, they will ensure your customers' wants are satisfied. If they are not, everyone in the business will spend a disproportionate amount of time disentangling them.

A process which is working well will produce few, if any, mistakes or delays and will not require much inspection or checking. A process which is working badly will create bottlenecks (piles of part-finished products, in-trays full of unprocessed invoices, long and unhappy queues at the check-out) or errors (rooms which are double-booked, under- or overcharging, burst carrier bags, a leaky roof . . .).

While a few of these outcomes may be the result of human stupidity, most will be the inevitable consequence of inadequate processes. Simply trying harder will not put things right. You will need to re-examine all the activities which make up the process, to see which parts of the system are at fault.

What do your customers want?

From the customer's point of view, the best process is one that:

9

There are channels along which resources flow

(a) works

(b) requires the least effort from him.

One-stop shopping is the ideal. For the business, that would mean just one person to manage and operate the process from start to finish. For the customer, it would mean just one person to contact for everything from placing an order, to checking progress, to negotiating settlement and arranging delivery. Such a completely integrated process would mean no functional specialisation for anyone. Instead, you would have flexible teams, working to do whatever was necessary to satisfy their customers. The feasibility of this will depend on the range of products or services supplied, the number and location of your customers, and of course the stability and skills of your workforce.

If you do decide you would like your customers to be treated this way, and assuming that your business is big enough to require some form of division of labour, there are two main options you might consider:

- You could organise yourself on a *geographical* basis and operate a separate process for each geographical area. Depending upon the market for your goods or services, this could mean establishing a European operation, one for North America, one for the Far East and so on. Alternatively, it might just mean separate groups of people working to service customers in different local postal districts. The members of each team would then design, make and deliver all your products to their customers, and also be responsible for all the other functions we have identified. Provided they have the necessary skills, knowledge and systems to enable them to do all these things efficiently and effectively, your customers should be satisfied.

  Such an approach demands a considerable amount of duplicated effort, with separate sales and marketing activities, separate production facilities, separate accounting functions and so

11

on. But provided everyone works to clearly defined principles and procedures, this can be very effective in getting and keeping everyone close to the customer.

- You could organise yourself on a *product* basis. Say, for instance, you install both double glazing and conservatories. Although you may buy both products from the same suppliers, you may find that, in the main, you are selling them to different customers. It might make sense to have some people specialising in windows while others concentrate on conservatories.

This will still mean some duplication of functions, and will be more difficult to apply where the products you provide are really interrelated. If, for instance, you produce skimmed and semi-skimmed milk, various types of cream, and ice cream, each of which either creates or uses by-products from the other, you might find it hard to separate your production facilities in the same way.

Simply dividing your labour either geographically or by product becomes less viable the more complex your products and the more sophisticated the skills required to produce them. However talented your employees it is unlikely that they will be equally good at all of the specialist functions we have identified. It may make more sense, therefore, to have one member of the team marketing and selling all your products to all your customers, while another looks after design and manufacture and a third keeps the accounts and looks after the administration.

If you opt for such *functional specialisation* you should be able to reap the benefits of increasing expertise in each functional area. To make it work, though, you will need to find some way of helping all three to keep their attention focused firmly on the customer. It is all too easy for those whose day-to-day contacts are primarily with their fellow employees to lose sight of what their customers really want. Before long, they may start developing systems and procedures which make their own lives easier while actually making things harder for your customers.

You can reduce the chances of this by making sure that the *total* process, and their part in it, is understood by everyone. As long as each person understands what outputs – in terms of information, ideas, components, product – they must provide within the business, to whom, when and in what format, you can build an internal chain of customers to help link your functional specialists to the real (external) customer.

How many levels of management do you want?

Each of the functions we have discussed calls for different skills. To complicate matters further, each also comprises a number of different elements:

- *Day-to-day practical skills.* The skills of the person who makes and decorates the cakes, welds the metal, makes up the beds, fits the carpets or does whatever else your customers are paying for – are central to the business. They add value to the raw ingredients and transform them into something your customers want. In the service or support functions, the skills of the person who writes the publicity leaflet, enters the data, makes out the invoices, collects the debts – are fundamental.
- *Organisational skills.* However good your cake maker is, if they run out of sugar, or have not got room in the oven, your business will not function smoothly and your customers will not be satisfied. Similarly, if you haven't bought enough sheets, or the laundry hasn't washed and ironed them, the beds in your hotel or guest house will not be made up, and again your customers will suffer. These are simple examples, but they highlight one of the things that can make the difference between delivering what your customers want, when they want it – and failing to do so.

13

Organisational skills

The bigger and more complex your business gets, the more vital these organisational skills become and the more broadly you will need to exercise them. Unless you *co-ordinate* activities effectively between functions, you could end up in real difficulties.

Suppose, for example, your sales and marketing person is offered some advertising space at an attractive rate. Believing she is doing the best job for the company, she takes it and goes to town with a glossy advertisement – for a product you can't make at present because the components are stuck at the docks or your storage or assembly facilities are inadequate. Instead of the expected boost in sales, all you will achieve is customer frustration. This is not a good basis for a successful business.

- *Planning skills*. Vital though day-to-day organisation and co-ordination are, they are not enough. Unless you (and your bank) are prepared to live from hand to mouth for ever, you must look to the future, too. In big organisations, entire departments are sometimes set up purely to advise the board on the future social, demographic, environmental, political and economic trends which may have a bearing on the company five or ten years hence, and to help them plan how best to respond.

In a small business, there is neither the time nor the need to attempt to be too sophisticated. Nevertheless, a bit of forward planning can help to avoid too much crisis management. And crisis management is at best pretty stressful and at worst yet another route to customer dissatisfaction.

Too much time spent on 'what if's' and 'maybe's' will not be productive. Too little attention to the future can be disastrous. The country is littered with the shells of businesses which assumed the boom would last for ever, or which failed to anticipate the change in pedestrian flow arising from the proposed re-siting of a car park or the decline in passing trade when a new by-pass opened. By developing a strategy for

15

future growth, taking account of likely changes, you are more likely still to be in business when the future comes.

So, whether or not you feel the need to divide the work into separate functions or geographical or product sections, you may feel it advisable to divide it into separate *levels* of activity. You could decide, for example, that the place for strategic planning is the board room, the place for hands-on practical work is the shop floor, and the intervening organisation and co-ordination should be done by supervisors and managers.

If you do decide this, you will, of course, be mirroring the structure of very many organisations, large and not so large. You may, however, be missing an opportunity. If you allow too much hierarchical demarcation, it will become self-sustaining and unable to adapt to changing circumstances.

If people on the shop-floor are told they must wait for the manager to get things organised and tell them what to do, they will usually wait. But if you ask them to take responsibility for getting themselves organised and to tell you what help they need, they usually will.

If you make it clear that the only people who are allowed to think round here are the bosses, the rest of your employees will use their brains in other ways – as school governors, organising charity events or doing a host of other things which actually demand quite a lot of planning and organising – outside work. If, on the other hand, you make it clear that it's everyone's job to come up with ideas for improving the business, at least part of that thinking power will be available to carry you forward.

It is this approach which is finally winning converts in the board rooms of even the largest companies. The days when big corporations had fifteen layers of management between the chairman and the shop-floor are, mercifully, over. In a small business with a relatively flat hierarchy, your best bet is to keep things that way. Resist the temptation to distance yourself from

16

the real work and hence lose contact with what your business is about. But do make sure you are not so busy minding the store that you simply don't have time to plan or to take advantage of new business opportunities.

Whatever decisions you have already made with regard to the overall shape of your business, keep them under careful review. Don't wait until after your first heart attack to decide you need to share the burdens of management. And don't assume that the structure that worked when you and your team were new to the game is the only one that will work now.

2 How many Players?

 If you were to divide your company into, say, three functions:

> operations
> marketing
> accounting

and employed just one person to do each at each of the three different levels we have identified:

> planning
> organising
> doing

you would have nine people doing nine completely different jobs. In practice, this would be completely unworkable for most businesses.

For one thing, unless your business process is very highly automated, you will almost certainly need a higher proportion of hands-on operations people than of anything else. These are the only people who really add value, not the financial planners or the marketing co-ordinators. For another, you may well find that one person can sensibly combine several different activties, across a number of functions.

So how do you decide how many people you need? There are no hard and fast rules to help you answer this question, but here are a few pointers which may be helpful.

- Think in 'man-hours', not numbers of people, to start with. There is no need to assume that all jobs will take exactly 39 hours per week (or whatever is the norm for a full week's work in your industry – we will discuss this shortly).
- Start by looking at the practical operations. How long does it take to bake each cake, service each room or produce each batch of output? Obviously there will be variations, but a reasonable estimate of the average will do as a guide. How many cakes do you sell in a month, how many guests do you have, how many customers? It sounds pretty obvious, but once you have multiplied one figure by the other, you know how many man-hours of operational activity (direct labour) you need.
- Now consider the support functions. How many man-hours of practical accounting, administration, advertising and so forth do you need per sale? This will probably be an even less precise calculation, but try to be as realistic as possible and, if necessary, monitor the work for a while to try to get a feel for the time spent. Again, multiply the number of man-hours per sale by the number of sales and you have your support function (indirect) man-hours.
- Add the direct and indirect man-hours together and multiply by what you consider to be a reasonable hourly rate for such practical work – including employers' National Insurance contributions. You will find some guidance on how to calculate rates in Chapter 6 and may, of course, want to introduce a higher level of precision into your calculations by using

So how do you decide how many players you need?

different rates for work in different functions.

- Now you know what your operational pay bill is likely to be – and you may not like the answer. If you don't, you have only three options:
    - speed up your operations
    - reduce your hourly rates
    or
    - go out of business.

  If you try to do anything else, you are simply deluding yourself.

- If you have got this far, the next step is to take account of the man-hours that will need to be devoted to planning and organising. Work at this level usually attracts a higher rate of pay, so you will need to adjust the hourly rate calculation accordingly.

  The man-hours spent on these activities are also less likely to be related quite so directly to the level of sales, so you may find it easier to work on the basis of simple ratios. One way is to analyse where time goes at present, for the people you currently employ.

  You might find that for every eight hours on the shop-floor, one hour goes on planning and organising. Or you might find something closer to a one-to-one ratio. Whatever it is, unless you can find ways of improving on it, you will need to build it into your calculations and multiply by the relevant hourly rate.

- By now you will have a feel for the total number of man-hours you will need per week or per month, with a rough idea of how these are distributed between activities, and an even rougher idea of how much they will cost. If you are an optimist by nature, you will probably have undercooked the figures a bit, so it may be a good idea to round them up before proceeding.

The next step is to consider how many 'full time equivalents' the figures represent. Just because *you* are prepared to work 12 hours

21

a day, seven days a week, 52 weeks of the year, do not assume everyone else is. You must take account of:

- *Holidays*. Most people will expect at least four weeks per year, plus Bank Holidays or time off in lieu.
- *Sickness*. Colds, flu and other mishaps will take their toll of even the most dedicated workforce. You will be very lucky to get away with fewer than five days' absence per person per year, and you might find it is closer to 15.
- *Standard hours*. For most of British industry, 35 to 40 hours represent a full working week. Extra hours usually attract premium rates of pay (overtime) and are therefore expensive. On the other hand, making extra use of the skills of those who are already experienced can be a lot cheaper than recruiting in extra hands at flat rates – especially if the peaks are relatively brief. There is a limit to what is sensible, though. If you expect too many hours for too long a period, you will find mistakes occurring through plain weariness. If you employ young people under the age of 18, the hours they may work are restricted by law. European legislation is likely to start phasing in a ceiling of an average of 48 hours per week over a four-month period, for all workers, by the end of 1996.

What are the jobs that need to be done?

Now that you are clear about the functions and activities to be performed, and the approximate numbers involved, you can start to define specific *jobs*. There is no such thing as a perfectly designed job. Almost all have their areas of frustration, boredom or ambiguity. But some are intrinsically more 'do-able' than others. Here are a few pointers:

- Try to strike a sensible balance between *specialisation* and *variety*. Up to a point, the more people focus in on one activity, the better they get at doing it. But only up to a point. Inserting one particular type of bolt, or packing one particular type of carton, all day, every day, gets very boring. When people are bored, their minds wander. When their minds wander, mistakes occur. So aim to include a range of related activities in each job, and to ensure that no activity is repeated too frequently.

- Try to include some tasks which are relatively *routine* and others which are more *challenging*, and perhaps some which involve working with others as well as some which are done in isolation. In particular, make sure as many jobs as possible include at least some element of contact with your customers.
- Wherever possible, let people '*see things through*'. This is usually better for the customer and is also much more rewarding for the individual. It may not always be possible for the person who bought a particular batch of material to make it up, load it onto the lorry, deliver and install the finished product. But it should be possible for him or her to have responsibility for checking the material's arrival in the store and for getting feedback from the operators about what it's like to work with.

 In most small businesses it is unlikely that anyone will be so far removed from the finished product that they think you spray panels rather than building motor cars. But it is quite possible for a hotel kitchen hand to lose sight of the fact that you are in business to delight your customers rather than to peel potatoes.
- *Take account of what happens elsewhere.* If you are going to have to recruit new people from time to time, for replacement or for growth, this will be easier if the jobs in your company bear at least some resemblance to those available in other companies. If you are the only person in the district who needs a software engineer who can write advertising copy, prepare your company accounts and erect marquees, you may not find yourself spoilt for choice when you try to recruit.

23

What about hours of work?

You know what the jobs are, and roughly how many man-hours you need for each. You are now ready to give serious thought to patterns of work. The main options are:

- Hire in *freelance or self-employed workers* when you need them. These people will not be on your payroll, and will be liable for their own National Insurance and Income Tax payments. (Unless they do this, and are in effect running their own business offering their services to a number of other companies, you could find they are deemed in law to be your employees after all. You will find more discussion of this issue in one of the other books in this series, *Keeping the Team in Shape*.)
- Hire in *agency personnel*. You will find details of your local employment agencies in Yellow Pages. As well as helping you to recruit your own employees, most have a register of people who are retained by the agency but who will work for other employers on a temporary basis. Any contract of employment is normally with the agency rather than the person using their services.
- Employ people on a *part-time* basis for a few hours per day or per week.
- Employ people on a *fixed pattern* of hours, to correspond with those when you are open for business.
- Employ people on *flexi-time* – ie agree the total number of hours to be worked in a month or a quarter, and the core time when all employees must be present (eg from 10.00 am to 4.00 pm). Leave employees to decide, individually or in work groups, what time they actually start and finish each day.
- Employ people on an *annual hours* contract – ie agree the total number of hours they will work in a year, and the money they will get in return, and then call on them to work when you need them.

- Employ people on a *shift basis* – either fixed or variable – to maximise machine usage, keep the process running, or service your customers around the clock.

Any of the employment options can be entered into on a permanent, temporary or fixed-term basis. We discussed the pros and cons of non-permanent employment in Chapter 1. Fixed-term contracts for periods of more than two years will entitle employees to the same treatment as permanent employees with the same service, unless they explicitly agree to waive their right to claim unfair dismissal or a redundancy payment.

Each of the above options has its attractions, and of course you can use a combination for different roles. There are a number of factors you may wish to take into account in deciding which pattern to adopt.

The amount of flexibility you need
If your business fluctuates widely at different times of the year, it will be simplest to hire in freelance workers, go to an agency, or recruit your own temporary staff. The drawbacks will be:

- *The need to make sure the legal basis is clear.* You don't want suddenly to find that the person you thought was paying his or her own National Insurance and tax bill is in fact legally your responsibility as an employee.
- *Cost.* Agencies have their own overhead costs to support, as, to a lesser extent, do the self-employed. Their hourly rates are likely to be higher than you would pay for your own employees.
- *Skill level.* If your work is specialised, you may find it takes too long to get an occasional freelance or temporary employee to perform to the required standard.
- *Acclimatisation problems* – of the kind discussed in Chapter 1, are likely to occur.

The next most flexible alternative, and one which overcomes the above problems, is the annual hours contract. Since you do not have to agree in advance exactly how the hours will be distributed, you can go quite some way to matching the available man-hours to the peaks and troughs in your business, while ensuring you always have experienced people on hand when you need them. The drawbacks are:

- Although you do not need to bring people in when there is no work for them to do, you will be paying them a constant amount throughout the year. Where you *do* save, is in not having to pay premium rates for extra hours, or guarantee pay for short time;
- Setting up such a contract is rather more complex than a standard hours arrangement, as both parties need adequate safeguards to avoid exploitation.

The number of people you want to be able to call on
If there are just one or two real peaks in the year when you need lots of highly skilled people on hand, having plenty of part-timers on the payroll could be the answer. Between them they will keep your business manned throughout the year. When you really need all hands to the pump, you can bring them all in at once. They will already be experienced and will not have got stale through working eight hours a day, day in day out.

There is a further advantage to using part-timers. To avoid claims of discrimination you must offer them pro rata the same pay and conditions as a full-timer, but you may save on National Insurance contributions. The percentage of employee earnings you must contribute increases as the employee's weekly earnings rise. For those whose earnings fall below the lower limit (£56.99 per week for 1994–95) you need pay nothing.

The main drawback is that not everyone wants to work part time. Most breadwinners need full-time earnings to make ends

26

meet. Although an increasing number are putting together their own portfolio of part-time work or becoming self-employed and working freelance, they are still a minority. If you can only offer a few hours work each week, it may not always be possible to recruit people with the skills and experience you need. One solution might be to share them with one or more other employers (perhaps including your competitors), but they may then not be available to work any extra hours for you as and when you need them.

The nature of your business
Your customers' expectations may dictate a particular pattern. The hotelier who wishes to cater to his guests' every need must have staff on hand at midnight as well as at 6.00 am. If you must be operational 24 hours a day, shifts will be the answer. Although you can still use freelance or agency personnel to work shifts, you may feel more secure establishing a regular team of your own people whom you know you can trust to work through the night without the same level of regular supervision as during the day.

Most people will expect to earn more for working unsocial hours, so this will put up your costs. This can be offset by the benefits of keeping expensive equipment fully utilised. It can certainly make sense to keep one machine working for 24 hours a day, rather than having three standing idle for a total of 48.

Opinions vary as to whether it is better to ask people to work fixed or variable shifts. In view of the difficulties of adjusting sleeping patterns, a permanent night shift appeals to some. Others prefer variety – three nights on, three off, followed by three days on, three off, followed by three evenings and so on. If you do set up a shift system, you will need to think carefully about how you communicate with, and maintain the involvement and loyalty of all three or four shifts, and how you make sure the same work standards are applied throughout.

Your employees' needs

Flexi-time can be particularly beneficial in crowded urban areas, where staggering starting and finishing times can save the amount of time employees spend travelling to and from work. It can also reduce the amount of lateness and absenteeism by enabling people to attend to family business, go to the dentist and so on outside core working hours.

Summary

These first two chapters have been about helping you to decide:

- how to divide up the work – by function, geography or product
- how many levels you need to cover the planning, organising and practical doing of the work
- how many man-hours of work need to be done
- how many people you would need, allowing for sickness, holidays and so on, assuming everyone worked full time
- how to group tasks together to form specific and worthwhile jobs
- whether you want to employ everyone for eight hours a day, Monday to Friday, or adopt some other pattern of work which better suits the needs of your customers, your employees and your business.

In the next chapter, we will assume that you have answered all these questions, and that you now have at least one job for which you need to recruit.

3 Getting Ready

 If your business has, up to now, been basically a family concern, you may never have had to think about venturing into the labour market with a view to getting a complete stranger to join your team. Even if you have already done some recruiting, you may well feel nervous at the prospect.

Whatever the basis of their employment with you, the people you recruit now will soon be 'insiders'. They will have access to at least some of your business secrets and ways of working. They may well see more of you than your family does.

For these reasons, as well as those we discussed in Chapter 1, getting it right could be critical to the future success of your business. In a large company, one selection error is unlikely to prove fatal. In a small business, it just might.

It must be worthwhile investing some time in planning your recruitment – not just to reduce the risk of errors but to increase the chances that your new recruit really will help your business to flourish.

In subsequent chapters we will look in detail at where and how you can attract the right candidate and how to make sure

Getting ready

you choose someone who will be an asset to the team. First, we will focus on the groundwork you must do in order to increase your chances of success.

Unless and until you know precisely what you are looking for, you are likely to waste time and possibly money going up blind alleys. There are two vital steps:

- describing the job
- working out what it takes, in terms of the skills, knowledge and abilities necessary, to do it effectively.

Before you can do either, some additional investigation will be needed to help you analyse what is required.

Analysing the job

In Chapter 2 we identified some of the factors to take into account when grouping tasks together. If you have followed the advice given there, the jobs in your company should be varied, interesting and fulfilling, with an appropriate mix of routine and challenging tasks.

So all you need to do now is to identify the detailed content of the job you wish to fill. In most large organisations, this would be done through a process known as *job analysis*. The outcome of the analysis would then be written up into a formal *job description* which could be used as a basis for a number of activities, including recruitment.

Your business may be small, and time may be at a premium, but it is worthwhile borrowing the basics. The approach will depend on whether the job has been done before, or is completely new.

If you are recruiting for an existing job you will have two very

31

useful inputs to your analysis. You can talk to the person who did the job before or to those who are already doing it. And you can talk to the people, inside and outside the business, who are their customers.

The purpose of your conversation with the job holder will be to understand:

- what *tasks* he or she undertakes and the *skills* and *knowledge* which are most frequently used – to help you work out what knowledge and skills to look for in the new recruit. This should be pretty straightforward, especially if you ask the job holder to talk you through a typical day, week or month. Another option is to ask them to tell you about the key processes in which they play a part, and to help you identify the actions required. For more complex jobs, a third possibility is to see if they can keep a special log book or diary for a little while, to record their activities. If this is impractical, perhaps someone else could 'shadow' them for a few days to observe what is involved.
- the *frustrations* and *satisfactions* of the job – so that you can look for ways of reducing the former – or at least forewarn potential recruits.
- the sorts of things the job holder believes could be done to increase the *effectiveness of the job* – so that you can re-examine it and how it fits with other jobs in the company.
- (if the job holder is leaving) their *reasons* for going. These may give you an insight into how it feels to work for the company, and help you form a view of the kind of people who are most likely to fit in and enjoy it.

  You may or not not feel it appropriate to try to persuade them to stay. Unless you really have been seriously underpaying, overworking or otherwise mistreating them – and can and will do better in future – it is sometimes best to leave well alone. Once people have made up their minds that the grass is greener somewhere else, let them go. If, as often happens, they find after a while that the old firm wasn't so bad after all, they'll be back. If you try to talk them out of finding out for themselves, they may always regret it – and you may find yourself beginning to doubt their loyalty.

Try asking questions in each of these areas. Keep a note of the key points. Remember, your aim is to get enough information to help you decide what the job is really all about and what it takes to do it well. The purpose of your conversation with customers and colleagues will be to understand:

- *where the job fits in.* What part does it play in the total business process? How does it contribute to the satisfaction of your customers' wants? What would happen if it wasn't there? Who would suffer? How? How else could their needs be met? Just occasionally you may find that the answers to these questions indicate that no replacement is needed after all. Usually they will help you to understand more about the critical elements of the job, the *key tasks* which must be carried out.
- the *attributes* which other people value in previous or existing job holders. By asking for examples of the sorts of things they do that work well, and of things that do not work so well, you will begin to build up a picture of what is needed.

  If, for instance, colleagues point out that mistakes in paperwork make their lives difficult, you might take it that attention to detail is important in the job. If you press them to find out the sort of mistakes which occur most frequently, you may establish that arithmetic errors are the real problem. From that you can deduce that you need someone who has the numerical skills to cope with the kind of calculations involved.

  Try to make sure each conversation focuses on the positive as well as the negative. It is all too easy to react to the things the previous job holder lacked by concentrating exclusively on them when it comes to looking for a replacement. In our example, unless you also discover that this particular person really helps customers to understand the product and its benefits, by explaining and demonstrating them clearly and patiently, you might recruit someone who is a mathematical genius but a lousy sales representative.

Remember, too, that the purpose of these discussions is to help you analyse what you need next time around – not to engage in character assassination of the person who used to do the job.

Listening carefully to the comments and ideas of the job holder, and of those who are part of the same process, will almost always provide wider and deeper insight into both the job itself and the attributes required. It can also ensure that the combination of tasks which go to make up the job can be rethought if necessary – before you start recruiting.

But what if it's a new job?

We will take it that you have identified a weak link in your business process. Somewhere along the chain from product design to customer, or in one of the supporting functions, you have decided there is something missing.

It may be that the relevant tasks are being carried out by someone as part of a bigger job. Or it may be that they are spread around a number of people, and no one has real responsibility for seeing them through. Or maybe you have suddenly realised that there is a whole function which just hasn't been happening. Whatever the reason, you have a gap you need to fill.

Your primary focus must be on the nature of that gap. Talk to people on either side of it. Identify those who are producing output which would logically pass to the person filling the gap. Talk to the people who would use the output produced by the person who fills it. The questions to ask will, in essence, be similar to those we explored in relation to filling existing jobs. The difference will be that people will have to use a bit more imagination and think a bit harder about their answers. Once they have given you the information you need, you can start to think about drawing up a list of what you will want the new person to do.

Describing the job

The last thing you want in a small, dynamic but, hopefully, growing company is a pile of paperwork – especially if the contents are likely to become set in concrete. Many large organisations have paid the price of an overly bureaucratic approach to drawing up job descriptions. They have found themselves growing increasingly inflexible and suffered repeated demarcation debates as employees decided to do only what was written down.

So you don't need a six-page document to describe each job. On the other hand, you do need a simple checklist to help you make sure you don't leave out anything important when you are talking to potential applicants or when you are trying to analyse the skills and knowledge needed to do the job. Your checklist should include:

- *Title*. You will probably want to use this in your advertisement or recruitment notice, so it should clearly convey the nature of the job. Some companies use fancy titles like 'customer service executive' when they mean 'sales assistant'. This may make those already doing the job feel good, but it can be very confusing for applicants.
- *Purpose*. Note down the main reason why the job exists. Is it 'to drive the van'? Or is it 'to deliver consignments of finished

35

goods, on time and undamaged, to customers throughout south-east England'? The latter gives a clearer idea of the real responsibilities of the driver.

- *Key tasks*. You don't need a detailed list of everything the job holder will do. 'Tidy the paper clips and the envelopes, count the pencils and order more paper' goes into too much detail. 'Run the office' is too general. 'Manage the stationery, provide a word processing/typing service for three people, set up and maintain the customer filing system (currently 300 customers) and route incoming mail and telephone calls to the appropriate person (currently 20 staff)' is probably as much detail as you would need to record for someone coming to help out in the office. *You* probably won't need to be reminded of the numbers, but must applicants like to get a feel of the size and scope of the job, and how busy they will be.

- *Conditions*. Hours and days of work, rate of pay, and particular circumstances such as a requirement to travel or spend nights away from home, outdoor or particularly noisy or hazardous work, should all be noted down. They won't necessarily go in the advertisement, but you must make sure you explain them at some stage or you may find your new employee doesn't last very long. (There's more on this in Chapter 6.)

Keep it simple, and to the point. Make sure you have covered all the issues raised in your discussions with previous or existing job holders. Don't be tempted to leave out tasks which you know are frustrating or difficult. Not everyone will find them so, and your new recruit will not thank you for sweeping them under the carpet.

Working out what it takes

If you don't know what you're looking for, you have very little chance of finding it. It is tempting to skip this stage, on the basis that 'I'll recognise it when I see it'. It is more likely that what you will do is fall for the most plausible and personable candidate – not the one with the skills and knowledge needed in the job.

So how do you translate your list of key tasks into a list of the skills and knowledge required for the position? One solution is not to try. If you want someone to manage your stationery, look for someone who has done it before somewhere else. If you want someone to do your word processing, look for someone who has a college certificate saying they have passed an exam in it.

This is certainly the quickest and easiest route – and lends itself readily to conversion to a clearly worded advertisement or recruitment notice. There are a few provisos we must make, though.

- Having done the same kind of work before does not necessarily mean that it has been done well – or at the right speed to make it cost effective. You need to be clear what that standard is, and how you will recognise it when you see it.
- Having passed an exam in something does not necessarily mean that the standard achieved in the classroom will automatically transfer to the work-bench, shop or office. While many qualifications are now linked to an assessment of competence through the system of National Vocational Qualifications (NVQs), if you are using different word processing software from your local college, for example, you could find yourself disappointed.
- Candidates with *identical* experience may not be attracted – unless you have something extra to offer, for example pay, conditions, travel, location, or future prospects.
- By insisting on previous experience you may rule out people who might very quickly master the work involved – and do it better than some of the experienced applicants. A classic

example is the 'housewife' who wants to return to work. She may have experience of a whole host of activities, from taxi-driving to budgetary control, planning and organising others. If you are only prepared to consider applicants with a relevant employment record, you could miss out.

For all these reasons, it is better to take at least a little time to analyse what you *really* need. Must your driver have an HGV licence and no endorsements? Will you expect him or her to maintain the vehicle? If so what will he or she need to know to do so safely? How much physical strength will be needed? What will happen if he or she gets lost or is rude to your customers? What other skills are needed?

Must your sales representatives be able to calculate discounts on the spot *and* be familiar with all the technical features and functional benefits that customers will look for in your product? Must your receptionist be able to operate a particular type of switchboard without losing calls *and* pacify irate callers when you are all out? This is where the time you have spent researching the job and the demands it makes will pay dividends. But however good the previous job holder and/or existing employees are, beware of the danger of 'cloning'. True, you are unlikely to make a serious error if you look for someone with the same sort of background, education, experience and approach to life as the last one. But you may not find anyone who *quite* matches. Even if you do, you may have missed the chance to bring in a really fresh set of ideas.

If the job you are trying to fill is really important to the future success of your business, it may be worth seeking help in identifying what you are after. There are a number of professional consultants who can help you to draw up a detailed profile of the behaviour or the personality and other attributes of the kind of person you need.

Usually it will be enough simply to approach the task in a

reasonably systematic way. An *employee specification* provides a helpful framework. You can compile one by answering the following questions.

Do you need someone who:

- has specific technical, legal, financial or other knowledge, or knowledge or skill in operating or managing particular machines, processes or procedures?
- has a particular level of physical strength or fitness, of manual dexterity or speed of thought? Where or how will this be applied? How sure are you that someone who lacked it would not be able to do the job some other way?
- is good with figures? What sort of calculations, from what sort of information, with what sort of equipment?
- is good at making decisions? What sort, in what time-scales, with what input, and what consequences?
- gets the best out of other people? In what context, individually or in groups, using what sort of approach – dictatorial or consultative, telling or coaching?
- always sees a job through? What sort of jobs, in what time-scales, with what resources?
- is good with words? Reading or writing, letters, technical reports, advertising copy or other documents? Speaking or listening, presentations or less formal encounters?
- plans and organises and prioritises? Their own work or other people's? How complex, in what time-scales?
- has creative ideas? About what, how often, how practical?
- works well within a system and/or likes to know the rules and keep to them – or someone who is comfortable with uncertainty or ambiguity?
- is quick to learn? What sort of things – technical, practical, theoretical? How – by doing, reading, observing?
- is able and willing to drive? What sort of vehicle, how far, how frequently, to what standard?

- is able and willing to stay away from home? How often, for how long, with what level of contact?
- is able and willing to work on their own, making their own decisions and getting on with the job?
- shares the same values and general outlook as you have – in so far as these relate to work and relationships with customers and colleagues?
- is flexible as regards working hours?

Once you have answers to all these questions, you have a template against which to measure candidates. This will help you to:

- prevent your prejudices getting the better of you. You are not looking for a man or woman, black or white. You are looking for a *person* who matches the template. This is important. The Sex Discrimination Act, 1975 and the Race Relations Act, 1976 make it illegal to discriminate on the grounds of sex, marital status, race or ethnic origin. Unjustifiably specifying a requirement which is less likely to be met by members of a particular group can discriminate indirectly. The more systematic and objective you have been, the better.
- draft a recruitment notice or advertisement specific enough to attract people with the right attributes, and to deter those without.

You are now ready to begin your search for someone to fill the gap in your team.

4   Attracting Talent

The first place to look for someone to take on new responsibilities is inside your existing team. This may sound obvious, but it is surprising how often employees get 'pigeon-holed' into what they are doing at the moment. Just because you have never seen Grace doing anything other than packing cartons, that doesn't mean she isn't capable of checking invoices or talking to customers. Just because you have never seen Michael doing anything other than driving the van, that doesn't mean he isn't capable of selling your product.

You may think this advice is coming a bit late in the day. Why spend the whole of the previous chapter talking about defining the job and what it takes to do it well, if the solution to your recruitment problem is staring you in the face.

The answer is that *unless* you have applied some of the disciplines outlined in Chapter 3, you are likely to get it wrong. It is all too easy to turn a perfectly competent van driver into a totally incompetent sales representative. Once you have done it, you and your employee are both losers: you because you will probably end up with no van driver *and* no sales rep; the employee

41

Attracting talent

because he will not only have lost his job but probably his self-esteem into the bargain.

Only by working through the process of systematically determining what you need, will you be in a position to match the skills and knowledge of your existing employees against your checklist. If you do find a good match, everyone gains. Even if you have to replace them in their old job, you may well find it easier to find someone capable of relatively less-skilled tasks.

You will certainly find it an advantage to have someone in the new job who already knows their way around the company – for all the reasons discussed in Chapter 1. And if your new sales rep has always hankered for such a position, without a promotion it might only have been a matter of time before you lost him anyway. Now he has the chance to broaden his skills, experience more variety, and perhaps take more responsibility and a pay rise.

So your first option when you have a job to fill is to look inside the company. Don't take it for granted that no one will be interested. Let people know there is a job to be filled and what you are looking for.

You can do this casually and informally when you are talking to people about other things. Usually the grapevine will do the rest. As long as you let it be known that you are prepared to discuss the position with anyone who thinks they would like to be considered, you may be surprised at who comes forward.

If you are not in daily contact with everyone, you may need to resort to slightly more formal means – perhaps a brief note for general circulation or to go on a noticeboard. Even if no one actually asks to be considered, at least you haven't kept anyone in the dark about your plans.

If someone does express interest, neither you nor they should assume that the job is theirs for the asking. You will both need to spend time assessing whether the move really is to your mutual benefit. That will mean following at least some of the advice in Chapter 5.

If it turns out that this is not a good move, for whatever reason, you need to make sure your employee understands why. If you appear to be turning down good applicants without proper thought, they (and their colleagues) will think twice about putting themselves forward again, and may even become disenchanted with their present job.

If you can't promote or transfer an existing employee, you have a number of other options. Which you use will depend on the nature of the job to be filled, the current state of the labour market and, of course, how much you are prepared to spend. We will consider these in turn, starting with the least expensive.

Word of mouth

Even if they are not interested in or capable of doing the job themselves, your present team may know someone who is. Encouraging them to talk to friends and relatives *can* be a very cost-effective way of attracting new recruits. It can be used for any type of work and is quick and easy. Some employers believe in it so strongly they even offer a bonus to existing staff who introduce someone who stays for a specified period.

There are three major pitfalls, all of which can be avoided with a bit of common sense.

- If all your present employees come from the same sort of background, you will miss the chance to bring in someone different. This could be a problem if, for example, they are all white and male. If their circle of friends and acquaintances is also white and male, there is a chance you're missing out on the benefits of a multi-racial, mixed-gender workforce.

  Your company may be too small to warrant much attention

44

from the Commission for Racial Equality or the Equal Opportunities Commission (which help to uphold the law against race and sex discrimination). But both have issued codes of practice which recommend that your choice of recruitment sources should be geared to attracting suitably qualified applicants from as wide a cross-section of the community as possible.

- If someone whom you value highly recommends a close friend or relative, you may be tempted to say 'yes' without really analysing whether they are capable of doing the job to the standard you require. Once you have asked for recommendations, you need to be careful that you and the present employee understand that there is no obligation, and no reflection on your employee if you decide not to follow their recommendation.

- If you do recruit someone on this basis, you need to be aware that 'keeping it all in the family' isn't always a good idea. Relatives *can* work very effectively together. Indeed, their shared involvement may mean they feel a higher level of commitment and loyalty to the business than either of them would on their own.

But there are risks. Especially if the two of them work directly together and without close supervision, it can be all too easy to turn a blind eye to each other's minor, or even major, lapses. At the extreme, they may even decide to work together against the business, systematically defrauding you.

Such cases are rare, and shouldn't deter you from sensible use of word-of-mouth recruitment. They should, however, be mentally noted and encourage you to avoid putting temptation in people's way.

The Job Centre

Recruiting from the Job Centre costs nothing. There is one in nearly every town. You will find the address of your local one in the telephone directory under 'Employment'. The staff are trained to help you define what it is you are looking for and to put you in touch with people who may be suitable. Whether you are looking for skilled or unskilled workers, this is a good place to start.

The only real disadvantage is that you may find you get too many applicants who have not been properly vetted by the Job Centre. Many of those who do apply are likely to be unemployed. That doesn't mean they haven't got plenty to offer. Indeed there may be a particular advantage in taking on someone who has been unemployed for long enough to qualify for the government subsidised *Training for Work Scheme*. You could offer a training placement rather than permanent employment. This means you provide a chance to learn; while your local Training and Enterprise Council supports part or all of the cost. Another excellent opportunity provided by the Job Centre is the 'Work Trials' scheme. Under this, you can take on a full-time employee for a three-week trial period. The employee continues to draw benefits for the three weeks, so that if either of you decide that the match between job and person isn't quite right – you haven't lost out by paying a salary for the trial period and the employee hasn't lost entitlement to benefits.

You may feel that the knowledge and skills you are looking for are more likely to be found in someone who is currently working – perhaps for one of your competitors. Even so, it will be worth talking to the Job Centre, making it clear that you are not prepared to see just anybody who thinks they'd like an interview. You have nothing to lose by having your vacancy on their noticeboard at the same time as you are pursuing other avenues.

The Careers Office

If you are happy to take someone straight from school, contact the local Careers Service. It may be possible to use the government's Youth Training arrangements to subsidise the cost of employing a 16- or 17-year-old, provided you are prepared to release them for the necessary off-the-job training and can give them a reasonable opportunity to learn on the job. The government has promised that Youth Training, linked to an appropriate National Vocational Qualification, will be offered to everyone under 18, so it could soon be difficult to recruit from this age group on any other basis.

Local colleges

If you need someone with a specific qualification, there may be no need to look further than your local college of further education. Most run courses on a very wide range of subjects, ranging from building trades to hairdressing and from motor mechanics to computer studies. Many of these help to develop very practical skills, and are again linked to National Vocational Qualifications. Most attract some more mature students, as well as school leavers. A telephone call to their careers office should get you on the right track.

Alternatively, if there is a university or one of the former polytechnics near you, you may be able to get someone with more advanced qualifications. Ask their careers officer whether courses include a placement period. You may be able to get someone in temporarily on this basis. If you need a permanent recruit, you can be sure that graduates of such programmes have at least a little practical experience as well as their theoretical knowledge.

You may be inclined to think someone like that would be too high powered for your small business. Remember that more than 30 per cent of school leavers now go on to higher education. If you need someone with a bit of thinking power and the ability to learn, you ought not to discount this as an entry route these days – especially if you recruit from a relevant vocational course.

Gate, doorway and window notices

These need not be expensive, but they can be effective. A tatty piece of cardboard stuck out in the wind and rain at the entrance to your premises may not have much impact. But a carefully worded, professional-looking board – perhaps at the entrance to the industrial estate or business park, or in your shop window or office doorway – can be useful, especially for casual or unskilled labour. You are not likely to find a qualified accountant by this route. You might well find shop-floor operatives or a driver.

Such notices are relatively cheap to produce, with letters on a magnetic board, or a series of carefully written cards (ideally encapsulated in film) for outdoor use. They vary from the unspecific 'Help Wanted' to a more precise list of job titles for current vacancies. The drawback is that you have no way of sifting applicants – and you probably won't be able to put enough information on the board to encourage self-selection. So you will need to have someone on hand to respond to the enquiries of passers-by.

That someone must have at least a little training. Not only should they be familiar with the job on offer and the skills required, they must also be careful not to say anything that might be construed as sex or race discrimination. The person who thoughtlessly tells a female enquirer 'Oh no, that's a man's job,' or who turns away enquirers from particular ethnic groups, could land you with a claim for sex or race discrimination. If you lose, it could cost you thousands of pounds.

Advertising

You can advertise in a bewildering array of publications, or on local radio or TV. All will charge you for the privilege – at rates varying from a few pounds to several thousand. National newspapers and radio or TV are generally too expensive to consider where you have only one or two vacancies to fill, and in most instances you will find the local paper does the job the most effectively. Unless you are prepared to pay relocation expenses, it's probably best to restrict your advertising to the local area anyway.

If you need people with particular skills, though – a food technologist, a software engineer, a quantity surveyor, it is worth searching out the relevant specialist periodical. You will find current information on such publications in *British Rate and Data*. This gives addresses, circulation details, advertising rates and so on. You should be able to find an up-to-date copy in your local reference library. If you advertise in these be prepared for the inevitable questions about relocation, though, as most of these publications have a national circulation.

When it comes to preparing the advertisement, you have several decisions to make.

- *What sort of advertisement* should it be – classified or display? Classified or 'small ads' are cheap but generally uninviting. Only those seriously looking for a move bother to study them closely. You can try to make yours stand out by spreading out the text, varying the type size and creating a bit of space within the column.

  For relatively unskilled jobs which you haven't been able to fill by other means, this may be the best bet. For more specialist positions, it may be worth investing in a larger, display advertisement. These give you a chance to section off part of

the page, and be more creative in your presentation.
- Should you *write it yourself* or employ an advertising agency? The latter need not be a lot more expensive, as most of their revenue will come in the form of commission from the publication where the advertisement is placed.

  If you have used an agency to help you with product advertising, don't assume they will be the best choice for recruitment. The skills are different and an agency that specialises in recruitment work is more likely to be able to give you sound advice on where to place the advertisement. Most agents will have an entry in 'Yellow Pages', but you may do better to ask around locally.
- *What should you say?* You can only answer this by bearing in mind the main purpose of the advertisement. That is, to enable the person who has the skills and knowledge you seek to recognise themselves and feel sufficiently attracted to the job to apply. You really don't want hundreds of applications. You only need one, so long as it's the right one.

To help achieve this, you need to put yourself in the candidate's shoes. What does he or she need to know in order to decide whether to apply? (The job description and employee specification should help you.) Look at the box opposite for a few do's and don'ts.

For a relatively simple advertisement that you want the paper to typeset for you, it is enough to write or type the text clearly – or even phone it through. Anything more elaborate may require professional typesetting and graphics from a marketing or advertising agency or graphic designer. They will pass the necessary images onto the newspaper in the appropriate format – for a fee.

DO

- Make sure the *job title* is explicit. Put it in the headline, in large type.
- Specify what you are *prepared to pay*. This need not be an exact amount – top and bottom limits, or 'negotiable circa £200 per week' are much better than 'salary according to age and experience'.
- Give as much *information* as you can about what the job entails. If the title is truly self-explanatory you needn't go into too much detail, but you must make sure candidates can see how they would spend their time. This is where your care in defining the job (Chapter 3) will pay off.
- Make it clear what specific *skills, knowledge and experience* you require. You needn't include the whole list, but make sure any that are essential are clearly spelt out.
- Give the *company name and address* and a few words about the *nature of your business*. Include only enough information to enable applicants to see the job in some kind of context. Overselling the company, or padding out the advertisement by waxing lyrical about its achievements isn't usually necessary.
- Make it clear *how, when and to whom* the application should be made, see below.
- Try to write in a style that reflects the *style of the company*. Unless you are very formal in your dealings with employees, use 'you' and 'we', not 'the successful candidate' and 'the company'.

DON'T

- Try to make the job or the company *sound more glamorous* than they are. It is a waste of your time to bring candidates along for interview under false pretences.
- Say anything that could amount to *sex or race discrimination*. Job titles like 'manageress', 'storeman' or 'Girl Friday' come into this category, as do references to the successful candidate as 'he' (or 'she').
- Use two words where one will do. It will cost you more and candidates will get bored.
- Try to be too *gimmicky*. A professional advertising agency *may* be able to produce an eye-catching headline or graphic. Amateur efforts often end up embarrassing their originators and putting off candidates.

Using an employment agency

Advertising can be hard work. Not only do you have to spend time creating and/or vetting the advertisement and deciding where to put it, there is no certainty that it will produce the right response. If it attracts too many replies, you will spend hours trying to sift them. If it doesn't produce the right sort, you will be back where you started – paying for yet another advertisement with no guarantee of success.

One way of avoiding this is to let a recruitment agency do the work for you. Although some agencies prefer to build up a relationship with companies that recruit regularly, others will be interested in 'one-offs'. Some specialise in particular types of job – computer personnel, drivers and fork-lift truck operators, secretarial or catering. Others offer a more general service – on either a permanent or temporary basis. You can find them listed in 'Yellow Pages', though recommendations through your business contacts may be safer.

The agency will charge you a fee, usually a percentage of the first month's salary, or a flat rate. Make sure you know the approximate size of the bill before you start.

Check whether they are likely to be able to fill the position from those on their books at present. If not, there may be advertising charges on top. Also check what happens if they recruit someone who doesn't work out. Most offer some sort of rebate, on a sliding scale, during the first few months of employment. This, and the fact that a properly briefed and competent agency can sift down to a tight shortlist, can make what initially seems like an expensive way of doing things more attractive.

To get the best from them, you will still need to do a lot of the ground work. If you don't know what you want, they won't be able to help you find it. So go along armed with:

- the job title and a brief description of the duties
- your employee specification
- an idea of how much you are prepared to pay the person

selected, plus any other relevant terms and conditions

- a view on how much you want the agency to do and how much you are prepared to do yourself – in terms of shortlisting and interviewing
- your questions about their method of operation and charging, and the length of time they expect it to take to fill your vacancy.

Whichever source of recruitment you are using, it pays to plan how candidates should apply, and how you will deal with them when they do.

Methods of application

There are six main options, each with advantages and disadvantages.

- *Calling in person*, perhaps on a specified day, will be quickest – but unless you have briefed the Job Centre or agency very thoroughly, there will be no chance to sift out the patently unsuitable.

   You can, of course, ask candidates to complete an *application form* on arrival. Unless the job requires a reasonable level of written skill or form filling, you should be prepared to help those who have difficulty completing it – especially anyone whose mother tongue is not the language on the form.

   Application forms in general provide a good and systematic way of gathering information to assess suitability. By asking candidates to sign to confirm the accuracy of the information they supply, you can also safeguard yourself against fraudsters. If you discover after you have taken them on that the information was false, you should be able to dismiss them without fear of legal retribution.

   Asking people to complete an application form may seem a bit bureaucratic. But a relatively simple one like that overleaf is quite quick and easy to fill in. You can get copies from Chancellor Forms (see Useful Addresses).

- *Telephoning for a preliminary discussion* is also quick and less time consuming, but requires someone able to conduct a telephone interview to answer calls – see Chapter 5 – and you will still need some written details later.
- *Telephoning for an application form* takes longer, and means some applicants may lose interest, especially those for jobs which don't normally involve much paperwork. It does, however, enable you to consider applications at your convenience.
- *Writing enclosing a* curriculum vitae *(CV)* will mean it is several days before you see any response. Those who are seriously looking for a professional or managerial job will probably have their CV typed up and ready to hand. Those who were simply attracted by your advertisement may be deterred by the need to prepare one. Candidates for less specialist jobs will almost certainly be put off.

  CVs also have the disadvantage that the candidate tells you what he or she wants to – rather than precisely what you need to know. This can make it harder to assess how well they really match your specification.
- *Writing to explain how you meet the requirements* will be easier for those not accustomed to preparing their CV. Unless you subsequently ask for an application form to be completed, you are likely to obtain only partial information about the candidate's background – the part he or she wants you to know. It will often be hard to assess much beyond handwriting skills and the capacity to write a business letter – neither of which may be particularly relevant to the job to be filled.
- *Writing for an application form* is also relatively slow, but once the completed forms arrive you will be able to compare similar information about each candidate, against your specification.

  Whichever method you choose, bear in mind the candidates' convenience and expectations as well as your own. This is equally important when you move on to set up your selection procedure.

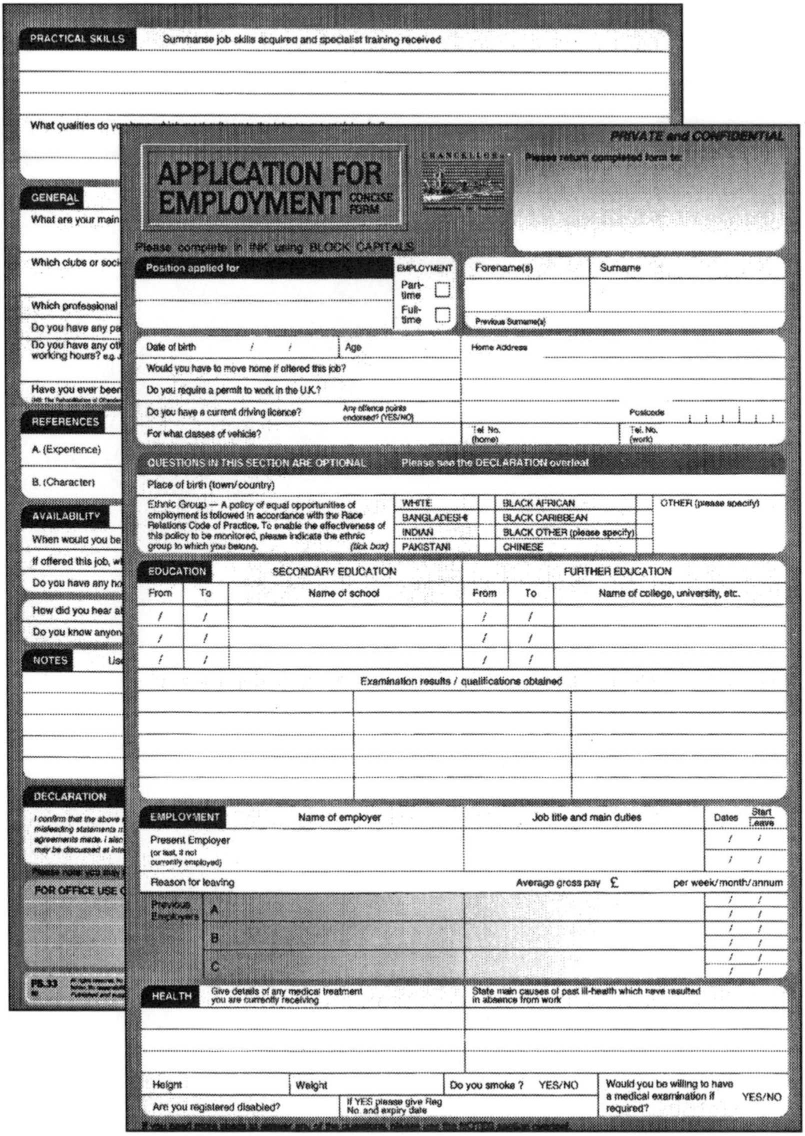

Back form (partially visible):

PRACTICAL SKILLS	Summarise job skills acquired and specialist training received

What qualities do y...

GENERAL	

What are your main...

Which clubs or soci...

Which professional...

Do you have any pe...

Do you have any ot... working hours? e.g. ...

Have you ever been...

REFERENCES	

A. (Experience)

B. (Character)

AVAILABILITY	

When would you be...

If offered this job, w...

Do you have any ho...

How did you hear a...

Do you know anyon...

NOTES	Lis...

DECLARATION	

I confirm that the above...
misleading statements...
agreements made. I also...
may be discussed at int...

FOR OFFICE USE...

FB.33

Front form:

CHANCELLORS

Please return completed form to:

APPLICATION FOR EMPLOYMENT CONCISE FORM

Please complete in INK using BLOCK CAPITALS

Position applied for	EMPLOYMENT	Forename(s)	Surname
	Part-time ☐		
	Full-time ☐	Previous Surname(s)	

Date of birth / /	Age	Home Address	

Would you have to move home if offered this job?

Do you require a permit to work in the U.K.?

Do you have a current driving licence?	Any offence points endorsed? (YES/NO)		Postcode
For what classes of vehicle?		Tel No. (home)	Tel. No. (work)

QUESTIONS IN THIS SECTION ARE OPTIONAL   Please see the DECLARATION overleaf

Place of birth (town/country)

Ethnic Group — A policy of equal opportunities of employment is followed in accordance with the Race Relations Code of Practice. To enable the effectiveness of this policy to be monitored, please indicate the ethnic group to which you belong. (tick box)	WHITE	BLACK AFRICAN	OTHER (please specify)
	BANGLADESHI	BLACK CARIBBEAN	
	INDIAN	BLACK OTHER (please specify)	
	PAKISTANI	CHINESE	

EDUCATION	SECONDARY EDUCATION				FURTHER EDUCATION		
From	To	Name of school		From	To	Name of college, university, etc.	
/	/			/	/		
/	/			/	/		
/	/			/	/		

Examination results / qualifications obtained

EMPLOYMENT	Name of employer	Job title and main duties	Dates	Start Leave
Present Employer (or if not currently employed)			/ /	/ /
Reason for leaving		Average gross pay £	per week/month/annum	
Previous Employers	A			/ /
	B			/ /
	C			/ /

HEALTH	Give details of any medical treatment you are currently receiving	State main causes of past ill-health which have resulted in absence from work

Height	Weight	Do you smoke ? YES/NO	Would you be willing to have a medical examination if required? YES/NO
Are you registered disabled?	If YES please give Reg No. and expiry date		

This form is reproduced with the permission of the copyright holder and publisher, Formecon Services Ltd, Gateway, Crewe, CW1 1YN

Assessing potential

5 Assessing Potential

 Whether you receive one application or one hundred, from people calling in person, telephoning or sending in written applications, your starting point when assessing them must be your employee specification (Chapter 3). Lose sight of this, and you are in grave danger of taking on someone who looks and/or sounds good, but who lacks some of the essential knowledge and skills that make the difference between success and failure in the job. You are also far more likely to allow yourself to be ruled by your prejudices – and land yourself with an expensive case of race or sex discrimination.

Handling telephone replies

If you have asked candidates to ring for an application form, all you need is someone to answer the phone, write names and addresses on envelopes, and insert the form ready for posting. If you have asked them to phone for a preliminary discussion, you will need to plan as you would for any other interview.

Have a checklist of relevant questions ready by the phone. Note each caller's replies on a separate sheet of paper, headed with their name, address, daytime and home telephone number. If you do decide to take their application further, this will at least make sure you know where to contact them. The notes of the conversation will also:

- help in planning a more formal interview later
- ensure that you have a record of what was said – in case anyone subsequently claims that you turned them down because of their race, sex or marital status.

Your main aim at this stage is to identify those candidates whom you are interested in seeing – and who are interested in seeing you. It is neither necessary nor appropriate to explore every avenue. Instead, select three or four key requirements, and see what the candidate has to offer. For example:

- If you need particular technical or professional knowledge and skill, explain this or remind callers that it was mentioned in the advertisement. Ask them to draw on their previous work experience or educational background to give you examples of when and where they have developed them.
- If you need someone who is a good planner and organiser, explain that this is so, and ask them to tell you about an instance where they had to exercise such skills.
- If you need someone who is comfortable working on their own, ask them about the set up in previous jobs and how they enjoyed it.
- If a pleasant telephone manner, clear speaking voice or articulate presentation are requirements of the job, note how the candidate matches up. Particular accents or dialect are much less important than the ability to make oneself understood in

an assertive, but not aggressive, manner.
- Ask the candidate what else, if anything, they feel they need to know at this stage. You don't want to invite a torrent of detailed questions. You do need to make sure the candidate stays interested.

Clearly the questions you select will be different for different jobs. You may find this a more fruitful line of enquiry than simply asking people to rattle off a list of previous employers, job titles and qualifications.

It does presuppose that the person conducting the interview is able to think of sensible follow-up or clarificatory questions and to answer routine questions from the candidates. It may not be necessary for them to evaluate candidates' replies in much detail, though – depending on whether you want to let people know the outcome then and there. Time permitting, there are advantages in waiting until you have a clearer picture of the size and quality of the response before issuing invitations to interview.

Either way, the conversation should end with thanks to the candidate for taking the time to call, and a clear indication of what will happen next.

Sifting written replies

Again you must be clear what you are looking for. If you need someone who expresses themselves clearly in writing, will have to complete printed forms as part of their work, or can spell correctly, it will be relevant to consider these aspects of their letter, form or CV. If the job will involve none of these things, concentrate on what they have said, ie their education, employment and practical skills, instead.

You are looking for indications that they have, or have not, developed the knowledge and skills you need. Some applications will stand out. They wil be the ones from people who are doing a similar job elsewhere. They should probably go on your 'to see' pile.

Check first, though, that their reason for leaving their present employer is sound. If they were sacked, it doesn't automatically rule them out – but it won't take them to the top of the pile. If they are looking for more money, promotion, or more responsibility, can you provide this? If not, there's not much point in proceeding.

Others are likely, for various reasons, to be less obvious contenders. They will be the ones whose practical skills appear to match those you seek, but whose employment or educational record lead you to wonder whether they are really up to your standard. If the 'to see' pile is looking a bit sparse, you will want to add the best of these, to find out.

Since the purpose of this exercise is to keep the 'to see' pile to a manageable number – bearing in mind that even the most rudimentary interview will take 15 minutes or so and you will need an hour or even longer to do a thorough job – resist the temptation to add people just in case.

Unless the response has been very poor, those who haven't provided enough detail to enable you to assess whether or not they match your requirements should be excluded. So should anyone who lacks an essential requirement – such as a clean driving licence for a job involving driving.

Those who indicate that they won't be available for interview or to start work when you need them will have to be rejected. So will those who indicate that they have other commitments which would prevent them fulfilling the demands of the job. (This does not automatically rule out people with responsibility for dependents – see page 66.)

People *over state retirement age* (now 65 for both men and women) can continue working if they wish, but they should check out the tax implications. *Children under 13* cannot legally be employed at all and the hours that can be worked by *young people under 16* are restricted by law. If any of your applicants are in this category you will need permission from the local education authority.

If any of your applicants need a *work permit*, this will not be worth pursuing unless the work is very specialised and you have been unable to attract any other suitable candidates from within the European Union. If you think it might be worth a try, consult the manager of your local Job Centre before proceeding.

People with a *poor health record* deserve your sympathy. But if this will be their first job after a prolonged or serious illness you may prefer to let a larger employer take the risk – especially as there are no rebates for the first four weeks of Statutory Sick Pay.

Those who are *registered disabled* are in a rather different category. If you employ more than 20 people you are required by law to take at least 3 per cent of them from the Employment Service's disabled register. This isn't always possible, as the number of registered disabled is insufficient to meet the quota, but a government subsidy may be available to help you employ a disabled person for a trial period. Depending on the nature of the work and of the particular disability, this could be worth a try. In jobs which are within their capabilities, most disabled people have good attendance records and are loyal and effective workers. If you have any queries about employing a disabled person, contact the Disability Employment Adviser at your local Job Centre or seek out your local Placing Assessment and Counselling Team (PACT).

Similarly, those who admit to having been convicted of a *criminal offence* should not automatically be ruled out. If the offence was relatively minor (ie the sentence was less than 30 months), and committed several years ago, it may well be what the Rehabilitation of Offenders Act, 1974 describes as 'spent'. That means it is illegal for you to take it into account.

Even if it is more serious or more recent, much will depend on the nature of the offence and of the work to be done. You would be foolhardy to employ a convicted embezzler to handle your accounts, unless you were very sure that he or she had been successfully rehabilitated. Employing him or her as a chef or a technician might be less risky.

Once you have got a manageable 'to see' pile, you can start notifying the unsuccessful. Depending on how confident you are of finding the right person among those you plan to take further, it may be a good idea to keep one or two of the 'nearly possibles' on hold until after the next stage in your selection procedure.

The interview

If you asked candidates to apply in person, you may already have a queue of people waiting at your door. If, on the other hand you asked people to write or telephone for an application form or take part in a telephone interview, you have a little time to plan how best to approach the interview itself.

The first task is to decide where to hold it. If you are recruiting unskilled labour and your specification is very basic, you can talk to people on the building site or the shop-floor. If you need anything more than physical strength and a reasonable level of reliability, you really need somewhere to talk in a bit of peace and privacy for at least part of the time.

It can be difficult to follow the thread of what a candidate has to say if you are constantly being interrupted by the telephone, customers, other employees or the sound of machinery. Later on, you will want to make sure your preferred candidates have a chance to see where they would be working, and to get the feel of the place – but that can wait.

If you don't have anywhere suitable, and are seeing a number of candidates, the local Job Centre may be able to let you have a room, or you could meet candidates at your premises and then take them out for a coffee if there's somewhere local. Conducting interviews in your car or van is another possibility, but you must make sure you are parked where people can see you, for your own protection. Such a cramped setting is far from ideal, as you really need to sit where you can relax a bit and see each other clearly.

Once you have decided, you must give candidates clear information about the date, time and place of the meeting and tell them how to find you and who to ask for. You can now give some serious thought to the questions you would like answered.

Your goals in the interview are:

- to determine whether the candidate is right for the job
- to determine whether the job is right for the candidate.

Both are equally important. As we saw in Chapter 1, recruiting someone who isn't capable of doing the job you want done can be expensive for you. But it's no use recruiting someone who doesn't want this sort of job, in your sort of company. He or she won't give of their best, and may not last long. Your aim must be to paint as clear a picture as possible of what is involved. That way there should be no nasty surprises later.

You are most likely to achieve these goals if you follow the guidelines below.

- *Keep your employee specification firmly in mind.* If you haven't already put your requirements into priority order, do so now. Are there any sensible trade-offs you can make? For example, could you settle for someone who isn't so creative themselves, provided they really are good at getting the best out of other people? This will help you decide the order of your questions and how much time you wish to devote to each area.

- *Think how best to word your questions.* Open questions – like 'how', 'how many', 'how often', 'what', 'with what results' – will take you further than direct or yes/no questions. Instead of asking 'Did you enjoy your last job?' – which invites a 'Yes' or 'No' in reply – try 'What was it about your last job that you enjoyed most?' This forces the candidate to think and to be specific.
- *Be ready to probe* the answers with more open questions: 'What factors influenced you?'; 'What happened then?'; 'How did your boss react to that?'; 'What was the customer's response?'
- *Plan the content.* Unless the candidate has failed to provide clear answers to the questions on the application form, don't be tempted to spend a lot of time going through it. You may want to check the sequence of jobs and reasons for moving – to see whether the pattern which emerges is one of a feckless wanderer, an ambitious self-seeker, or a logical progression. You may also want to investigate any gaps in the sequence – which could hide a period of illness, unemployment, moonlighting or a spell in prison not declared on the form. Beyond that, simply retracing their steps will take too long and not be sufficiently focused on the attributes you are looking for.

  Aim to keep the discussion as practical as possible. People who wish to entertain you with their theory of the meaning of life may be all very well in the pub. In an interview you need hard evidence of what they can and can't do.
- *Always request specific examples* and, wherever possible, a practical demonstration. (You will find some ideas on the latter in the next section.) Don't just ask whether the candidate, has or hasn't done, does or doesn't enjoy, something. Follow up with 'Can you give me an example of that?' or 'Could you tell me about a particular instance?'

  Never settle for generalisations like; 'Oh yes, I'm very used to dealing with the public' or 'I've got lots of experience of managing complex projects'. Ask 'Can you tell me about a specific occasion when you found a member of the public particularly difficult? . . . What exactly happened?' or 'What is the most complex project you've managed in the last year? . . . Tell me precisely how you handled it.' You will find that by using words like 'specific', 'exact' or 'precise' you can get the candidate to focus rather than waffle.

- *Aim to get a balanced view.* If the candidate has given you an example of a customer who was clearly satisfied, ask 'Can you think of a time when a customer didn't go away happy? . . . Tell me about that.' If you have talked about a project that clearly met its objectives, ask 'Can you think of one that *didn't* go so well?'

- *Anticipate the candidates' likely questions.* These can vary from specifics like 'When would you want me to start?' or 'How much holiday would I get?' to broader issues such as 'What sort of prospects are there if I show I can do *this* job?' Your answers will have to be factual – you are expecting the candidate to be precise and honest, you must be too.

- *Be alert to unspoken clues.* You *may* be prepared to employ someone with a drink, food or drugs problem or who is HIV-positive. If you'd rather not, you need to be aware of some of the possible signs. Candidates who stagger in reeking of drink are relatively rare. The indications are usually more subtle.

But you cannot assume that someone who is very thin has AIDS or is anorexic, any more than you can be certain that shaky hands indicate drug abuse or that sweating palms or bloodshot eyes prove the candidate is an alcoholic. Nor can you assume that anyone with none of these symptoms is clear of problems.

What you *can* do is to home in specifically on questions such as 'How many times in the last year have you been late for work?' or 'Have you missed work (or been unable to get out) for any reason other than those shown on your application form?' If you are really concerned, you can be more to the point – 'There are a few direct questions, not on the application form, which I ask everyone. Have you ever, or do you now, use drugs of any kind? How often do you drink alcohol? Have you ever been breathalysed?'

None of the answers will be conclusive, and you may upset a few genuine candidates by asking. You must weigh up the risks. If you don't ask the candidate, you may still be able to check with his or her referees later, see next section – or ask them to undergo a medical examination.

- *Don't make a habit of delving into candidates' private lives.* You are interested in their ability to do the job – to the required standard, usually for a specified number of hours. If a woman happens to disclose that she has young children at home, don't dive in to demand to know who looks after them or what happens when they're sick. Instead make it very clear what demands the *job* will make, and ask for evidence that she can and will satisfy them.

This will obviously be easier if she is already working somewhere else. You can ask her about her attendance record. If she is hoping to come back to work for the first time, you can ask what difficulties she believes she may face in meeting your requirements. As long as your requirements are reasonable, and not trumped up to deter her, you can form a judgement as to whether she is, or is not, likely to fulfil them.

The same sort of rules apply when dealing with *all* applicants. Try to make sure you follow a similar line of questioning with all of them. *Never* ask 'men only' or 'women only' questions. Even if you and your partner have agreed that 'a woman's place is in the home', do not impose this belief on others. Even if the last member of an ethnic minority group you employed walked off with your takings, don't assume that everyone from the same group is likely to do the same. If you are worried about honesty, check it out for everyone, not just those you mistrust. To do otherwise lays you open to claims of sex and race discrimination. It also means you could miss out on some very capable potential employees as a result of sheer blind prejudice.

- *Be prepared to listen.* Keen as you may be to tell the candidate about your business successes and your expansion plans, that can come later. There is no point identifying all that you need to know about the candidates and then spending half the interview talking about yourself. Give them time to think. Nod and look encouraging when they pause – don't interrupt or jump in with another question. Make notes if you can, perhaps using a copy of your specification as a framework.
- *Check that you have understood.* Every now and then try to summarise what the candidate has said, and then check out any areas that aren't clear. This should help you to avoid getting side-tracked and to remember what was said.

If you follow these guidelines you should uncover a lot of information about your candidates – information which should all relate to your employee specification. Before you attempt to make a decision, there may be a few more specifics you want to check.

Before, during or after the interview, you can ask candidates to provide a sample of their work or arrange for them to undergo tests. You can take up references, for some or all of the candidates. Or you can decide to give someone a trial before confirming their appointment. We will consider each in turn.

Work samples

The easiest way to check whether prospective delivery drivers can drive your van safely and reliably around your delivery area without getting lost – is to ask them to drive you round in the van, perhaps calling in on a few customers on the way. (It will be wise to check their driving licence and your own insurance first.)

The quickest way to check whether prospective nursery staff know a hydrangea from an azalea and can transplant a shrub without killing it – is to walk with them around your garden centre. Have them talk to you about the plants, and ask them to move one or two for you.

The simplest way to check whether prospective chefs can make an omelette or a pavlova – is to invite them into your kitchen.

The best way to check whether prospective designers can take a rain-soaked sketch and turn it into a professional drawing, or whether prospective secretaries can take some scribbled figures and a few notes and turn them into a specification – is to ask them to do it.

The examples could go on and on. All are based on the principle that if you really want to know whether or not someone is competent to perform key elements of the job to the standards you require, the best way is to let them show you what they can do. This may not prove that those who *do* perform to the required standard will automatically do so, day in, day out, should you employ them. But it will help you to identify any who simply do not have what it takes.

There are drawbacks of course:

- If you need candidates to be competent in more than one task, devising and obtaining work samples for each aspect can become very time-consuming – for you and the candidate. For you, there may be some compensation if you are able to use the output produced – the omelette, the drawing or the specification. This rather depends on the quality of the work. If you overdo it, or fail to explain what you are doing and why, some of your candidates may decide there are easier ways to get a job.
- If the task is one which requires some initial training –

knowledge of your particular products or of the layout of your premises, skill in using a particular machine or familiarity with a particular home-grown system, you will have to spend some additional time teaching candidates the basics.

This will be particularly crucial if candidates might otherwise be put at risk. The old building trade ploy of placing a bag of cement on the candidates' chair and expecting them to remove it – seems like a good way of assessing whether they have the strength to do the work. It could backfire, though, if someone who had not been trained to lift suffered an injury.

- Unless you take plenty of time and care explaining to candidates what is required, you could find you are indirectly discriminating against candidates whose first language differs from your own. Given more time and clear instructions or a demonstration, they may be perfectly capable of performing to the required standard. If you assume they are not, on the basis of a hasty briefing for an ill-devised test, you could lay yourself open to a claim of racial discrimination.

One way of reducing the impact of some of these problems is to ask candidates to bring their own work samples with them. In some fields this is a standard practice. Graphic designers, for instance, will expect to show a portfolio of their work. The risk here is that you have no way of knowing whether all the contents are genuinely theirs. It is also a problem where work is actually the property of a previous employer.

Work samples give you the chance to judge for yourself what someone is capable of. Even if you and your candidates are prepared to take the time and trouble to use them, there will be aspects of some jobs which cannot readily be assessed by such means. Anything which involves a prolonged period of training, or a significant level of involvement with customers or other employees, will be hard to cover. In such cases, you have three other options.

Formal tests

Psychologists have devised a number of ways of assessing the personality traits and patterns of thought and mental and physical aptitudes which make us what we are. Such *psychometric tests* are strictly *not* for amateurs.

If you are trying to fill a very important or complex job, and don't feel you will be able to assess candidates adequately using the methods so far outlined, try talking to a reputable employment consultant. They should be able to offer you some more sophisticated ways of predicting how candidates are likely to perform. Since most of these require specialist training to administer and interpret, such services do not come cheap.

Nor, of course, are they necessarily much more reliable than a well-constructed interview and work sample. For one-off recruitment assignments it is not easy for consultants to gauge exactly what level of performance on a given test is really needed to meet *your* requirements. Their assessments will tend to relate to norms for the population at large. The real benefit of such methods tends to come when relatively large numbers of people are recruited and can be followed up over a long period.

References

Some applicants sound a bit too good to be true. All are likely to be trying hard to put a positive complexion on what they have done. For particularly sensitive areas, like honesty, drink, drugs or other problems, and for those aspects you haven't been able to explore in other ways, references can be a useful additional source. Use them either to help you decide, or as a check after you have made up your own mind who is the best candidate.

References from previous employers are of more value than personal or character references. Most people know *someone* who thinks well of them, though if the referee has some standing in the local community – especially a teacher, doctor or other professional person, they are perhaps less likely to deliberately mislead.

If the person named as a referee for experience is not the immediate past employer, it is worth asking why. Often it will be because the candidate is still employed and doesn't wish to alert his or her boss until another job has been offered. In that case, ask if you can contact the one before. If that is *not* the reason, ask the candidate for permission to contact their last boss.

Consider making any offer of employment subject to a satisfactory reference from their present employer. If this subsequently proves unsatisfactory and is received within a reasonable time, you will be able to sack the employee if you want to. That may not be much consolation if you have just spent time getting him or her settled in.

It is not good practice to contact referees without the candidate's permission. The candidate, in turn, should have sought consent before putting names and addresses on the application form.

Wherever possible, telephone referees with some prepared questions. If contacting a previous employer, try to make sure it is the candidate's immediate boss you are talking to.

Your questions should include:

- confirmation of the dates of employment and the nature of the duties performed
- details of number of days' absence, comment on punctuality
- observations on work performance and general conduct
- their reason for leaving and the likelihood that they would be re-employed.

If the answers don't tally with the information supplied by the candidate, double-check. Say something like: 'That's interesting. I had understood he left you rather more recently that that . . .' or 'You haven't mentioned it, but I understood she did from time to time get involved in handling cash, is that so?' Make all your questions as specific as you can 'How accurate was his figure work?' 'How often did you receive complaints from customers?' 'Were there ever any indications of drug or solvent abuse?'

Remember:

- Some employers prefer not to implicate themselves by giving a bad reference.
- Some employers will be satisfied with standards of work and conduct a good deal lower than yours.
- Some employers will be glad to get rid of a problem employee and may decide to be 'economical with the truth'.
- Some employers will have lost their records, forgotten the employee, or muddled him or her up with someone else.

Be alert for signs of any of these – and be prepared to use your own judgement. Even if someone does mislead you and you suffer as a result, the scope for legal redress is very limited.

Trial periods

However carefully you have approached your selection, you can never be certain. Offering the job for a trial period gives you the chance of an extended work sample. This can have advantages for you. You may decide to withhold service-related hoidays, any pension arrangements and fringe benefits until after the completion of, say, a three-month trial. That may reduce your costs, and make you feel less tied. It should also prompt you ro review progress regularly, especially during the first three months, to your mutual benefit.

In practice, it achieves little else. Unless you were acting on the basis of trade union activities, race or sex, you could sack the employee in the first two years anyway without having to prove you were acting reasonably. If the new recruit is to have any real chance of success, you will have to spend some time in the first few months helping him or her to get to grips with the job. Doing it half-heartedly will be a waste of time for both of you. For the employee, a trial period may be quite unappealing, especially if they are giving up another job to come to you.

Whether or not you think there is merit in proceeding on a trial basis, you are now in possession of as many facts as you are likely to need. You should be ready to make your decision.

Clear winner

6 Signing up

One of your applicants may by now have emerged as a clear winner. Even so, it will be worth spending a few moments reflecting on all the information you have gathered, to ensure you really do offer the job to the best candidate.

Review your employee specification. Rate each candidate against each item. You can use a scale from one to five, or 'above/below/meets required standard'. Challenge each rating. On what evidence is it based? Where did you get it from – the application form, interview, work sample, references?

Look down the list. If one candidate scores high on, say five out of six requirements and very low on the sixth, you may be tempted to take a chance. If the sixth item is critical to success in the job, you may do better to opt for the person who scores slightly lower across the board – as long as they at least meet your standard on each.

Remember, too that getting someone who is overqualified can be almost as bad as someone who is lacking in key areas. Unless you can expand the job to make use of their talents, they may quickly become frustrated.

What if no one meets the required standard?
You can:

- settle for the best of a bad lot – and recognise that you will probably have to spend more time training the newcomer than you had bargained for. If the shortfall is in an area which is difficult to improve by training – like honesty – this is not a wise option to take.
- retrace your steps until you find a better way forward. Was there anyone you rejected along the way who might be worth a second look? Was the advertisement worded as well as it could have been? Was the brief to the Job Centre/agency clear? Was your specification really relevant to the job? Was the job itself clearly defined? Should you rethink the job – or even whether you need someone at all?

Whatever the outcome of your deliberations, make sure you keep a few notes about your conclusions. Use the application form or a separate sheet of paper. Record the key points which helped you to make up your mind about each candidate.

Don't be in too much of a hurry to throw away the paperwork for those who are unsuitable. There is just a chance one of the applicants, or someone acting on their behalf, may want to challenge your decision on grounds of race or sex discrimination. This will be a lot easier to refute if you have clear notes, made at the time of selection, recording your reasons for rejection. Clear them out every six months, unless you might want to consider them for another vacancy in future, if your first choice fails to match up to your expectations.

Contacting the candidates

You know who best matches your specification. You need to

decide whether to telephone, write, or make an offer on the spot.

For jobs which are typically paid by the hour or the week, there is definitely no need to waste time writing. You will have to put all the details on paper soon anyway, and you don't want to risk losing your chosen candidate. For other jobs, a phone call gives a sense of being wanted, and can get the relationship off to a good start, though candidates may want you to confirm the details in writing before giving notice to their present employer. The next section will help you to decide what the terms of the offer should be, and how to capture them in a written statement.

As soon as you have an acceptance – but not before – get back in touch with any candidates who are still waiting to hear from you. Thank them for their time and trouble. You may want to employ one of them at a later date, so try to leave things on a positive footing.

The terms of the offer

You are about to make an offer which, when accepted, will form the basis of a legally binding contract of employment. Any promises you make must therefore be honoured or you will be in breach of contract. It makes no real difference whether the promises are in writing or oral, and things you said at interview or in your advertisement also count. Written promises are of course easier for an employee to prove.

To start with, you will need to be clear who you are. This sounds obvious, but it is important that the employee knows who they are actually working for. If you have registered a number of different companies which is the relevant legal entity? Also make sure you have got the employee's name right, to avoid confusion.

There will be at least ten main terms, and others that you may feel important to get straight from the outset. Thinking about them all now will help to make sure you don't put anything in the offer which you don't really mean.

1. *Job title and main duties.* You need to be reasonably specific about what you want the employee to do. If the job title is self-explanatory there is probably no need to elaborate. If there is room for interpretation, a very brief list of the main types of activity involved – eg 'cleaning and general workshop maintenance' – should be enough. If you have followed the guidance in Chapter 3, this part should be easy.

2. *Place of work.* If the job is based in one location, where is that? If you need the employee to work in different locations or to travel in the course of their work, what is involved? Will this be in their own or a company vehicle, who is responsible for insurance, maintenance, fuel costs, etc, and what is the procedure for handling expenses? If the employee will work outside the UK for more than one month a year, you will need further details of the relevant terms and conditions.

3. *Start date.* If you offer employment, and hence payment, from a certain date, you may have to pay compensation for any postponement. Take particular care around Bank Holidays. Don't accidentally start someone on Christmas Day or you may have to pay for the whole holiday before they've actually done anything at all.

   Try not to choose a date when you or other key staff will be too busy to spend a little time with your new recruit. Agree the date with the employee, and allow time to serve appropriate notice with the present employer.

4. *Date on which continuous employment begins.* This will only differ from the start date if your new employee worked for an associated company or one you have just acquired.

   If the employment is only intended to be temporary, this should be clear. If employment is due to end on a fixed date, when is this? If there is a trial period involved, how long, and are there any conditions relating to it?

5. *Rate of pay and pay interval.* You must decide whether to pay in cash, by giro or credit transfer, weekly or monthly, and what the basis of calculation is to be. And do you pay in advance or in

arrears? You will find more detailed discussion of the options in one of the other books in this series: *Getting a Result*.

Here it is enough for us to note that, in the larger small businesses, the trend is towards monthly payment by credit transfer – which is safer and, unless you are a cash business, easier than cash. As far as the basis of calculation is concerned, this may be related directly to *output* – so much per piece made or item sold – or to *time worked* – so much per hour, day, week or year – with or without premium payments for overtime. You can, of course, combine the two, and may decide in addition to pay either an individual or group bonus related to sales or profit.

Whatever you decide, try to avoid overcomplicating the calculation. Also bear in mind that too much emphasis on 'pounds for effort' can eventually mean that people are reluctant to put in any extra effort without extra pounds, and too much emphasis on 'pounds for output' can lead to a 'quantity not quality' mentality. This may not be what your customers want.

Remember, too, it is important that your new employee is offered terms which are compatible with those enjoyed by your existing employees. These will probably be the main determinant of the actual level of pay you offer as well. If the post is a specialist one, you may need to gauge the local going rate by looking at advertisements for equivalent positions in the local paper, or consult the manager of your Job Centre.

6. *Hours of work.* Try to be as specific as possible. If you have a standard working week this will be quite straightforward. If you are going to ask the employee to work to the flexible or annual hours arrangements we discussed in Chapter 2, you will need to let them know how this works.

   Bear in mind that those who have worked for you for more than one month and whose employment will be for more than three months will be entitled to a *guarantee payment* for days when you are not able to provide work for them to do. Although this only applies for five days per quarter, and there is a legal maximum payable, it is better to err on the side of caution. If you will normally need someone for 30 hours per week but may occasionally need them for 35, make sure the offer, and the subsequent pattern of hours worked, makes it clear that 30 hours is the norm.

7. *Holiday entitlement.* This, too, will have to be compatible with any arrangements you have made for other employees. Have you

decided to shut up shop altogether at certain times? Is the employee to accrue days' holiday in return for weeks or months of completed employment?

Whose permission is required, how much notice must be given and are there any restrictions on the timing of holidays? You can specify that no holiday may be taken in the month before Christmas or at the height of the tourist season – or whenever your peak trading periods are. Does your trade or service require cover over Bank Holidays? You can also decide that all holiday must be taken in the year in which it is earned. That way you won't suddenly find yourself having to recruit temporary help to cover someone who has built up seven weeks of entitlement and wants to take them all at once.

Although the employee is only just starting, decide what will happen to accrued holiday when the employee leaves. Will you pay in lieu?

8. *Entitlement to sick pay and pensions.* Again, you will find guidance in other books in this series to help you decide whether to offer these. If they are to form part of the terms and conditions of your new employee, you must make sure the basis is clear from the outset and that the employee is informed of any rules governing, for example, the reporting of sickness or other absence. You must also let them know whether the employment is covered by a pensions contracting-out certificate.

9. *Length of notice.* The amount you must give to the employee is laid down by law. The amount he or she must give to you nominally follows the same pattern of one week for each year of service up to 12 weeks. In practice it is usually impossible to enforce more than one month's notice from employees, though many contracts for senior managers do specify longer. If you think you might want to pay in lieu of notice when the employee leaves, make your decision now. For those who have access to company secrets or direct contact with customers, there can be advantages in making a clean break as soon as they are no longer committed to your business.

10. *Details of any relevant collective agreements.* If you have entered into any agreement with a trade union which affects the terms and conditions of this employment, you must advise the employee.

If you employ more than 20 people, you will also have to have written details of your disciplinary rules and disciplinary and grievance procedures – see *Keeping the Team in Shape.*

Rather than trying to capture all this in an offer letter, which will inevitably become somewhat legalistic, it is best to write something much briefer and more welcoming. You should include everything that you think may influence a decision to accept – but if some areas are still open to negotiation, invite your prospective employee to call to discuss them.

As a guide, the job title, hours, place of work and an indication of pay and main benefits ought usually to be mentioned. You can either suggest a start date or ask the employee to telephone to agree one. Make it clear that you very much hope they will decide to accept.

Invite them to call you with any queries or worries – and to confirm their acceptance.

Tell them, either in the letter or when they call, about anything you want them to bring with them – tools, birth certificate, P45, bank account details, etc. If you provide any workwear or uniform, check their size and get it ordered. You will also need to let them know when and where to report on their first day and maybe even details like what to wear or where to park.

If the employee does try to negotiate an improvement in the terms you have offered, you will need to be clear how far you are prepared to go. Don't risk upsetting all your existing employees, but do look for ways of reaching a mutually acceptable solution. You want the new recruit to join feeling positive.

Once the terms are agreed you should record them all in a *Statement of Employment Particulars.*

You can use the pro forma below – obtainable from Chancellor Forms at the address on page 89. You don't *have* to give this to the employee before he or she starts work, but anyone who will work for more than eight hours per week and whose employment lasts for more than one month is entitled to both a principal and supplementary statement like those shown. These *must* be issued within two months of the beginning of employment, so getting the paperwork organised from day one – or before – will save time later. (Any subsequent changes must be notified, in writing, within one month of coming into effect.)

Introducing the new recruit

Once the start date is settled, you must make sure you are ready to receive the newcomer.

- Collect together all the correspondence you have had with him or her – including the application form, the offer letter if you sent one, and the statement of employment particulars. These will form the basis of a personal file for the employee. If you wish to summarise this information for easy access, and record other relevant items as they occur, you can use an *employee data folder* – available from Chancellor Forms.
- Tell everyone – especially those who will be working with or helping to train the new recruit.
- Plan the first few days/weeks. You won't need a complicated induction programme. You will need to make sure the newcomer meets everyone and has a chance to find their feet.

There are a few things you *must* make sure they understand from the start:

- the location and use of *first-aid equipment* and *fire extinguishers*, and what to do in the event of a fire
- other *essential safety information* – eg areas where protective clothing is required, procedure for handling hazardous substances or equipment
- rules about *smoking*, *timekeeping* and *breaks* and what to do if taken ill
- the location of *essential facilities* – toilets, rest room, where they can eat

82

STATEMENT OF EMPLOYMENT PARTICULARS

Part 2 of 2 *Supplementary Statement*

The following
of y

SICKNESS and/or INJURY
(state any terms and conditions relating to incapacity for work due to sickness or injury, including any provision for sick pay. Alternatively attach a document which gives the particulars or state where such document can be easily located by the employee)

PENSION ARRANGEMENTS
(state any terms and conditions relating to pensions and pension schemes. Alternatively, attach document which gives the particulars or state where such document can be easily located by the employee)

LENGTH OF NOTICE
(state the length of notice the employee is obliged to give and entitled to receive to terminate the contract of employment)

DISCIPLINARY RULES & PROCEDURES
(state any disciplinary rules and procedures applicable and the manner in which any application should be made if dissatisfied with any disciplinary decision. Alternatively attach a document which specifies such rules or procedures or state where such a document can be easily located by the employee)

GRIEVANCE PROCEDURE
(state the manner in which an application for redress of a grievance should be made. Alternatively attach a document which sets out such procedure or state where such a document can be easily located by the employee)

COLLECTIVE AGREEMENTS
(state any collective agreements which directly affect terms and conditions of employment including, where the employer is not a party, the persons by whom they were made)

Wh

Signature for
and on behalf
of EMPLOYER

STATEMENT OF EMPLOYMENT PARTICULARS

Part 1 of 2 *Principal Statement*

EMPLOYER'S NAME and ADDRESS

EMPLOYEE'S NAME and ADDRESS

The following are particulars of your employment as at Date

(In boxes marked * enter YES or NO)

Place of work is the same as above address *

Employee Ref.

Place of work if different
(or state 'various' if employee is required or permitted to work at various places)

Note 1 applies *

PLEASE READ NOTES 1 - 5 OVERLEAF

Employment began (date)

Continuous employment began (date)
(if any employment with a previous employer is included)

Period employment expected to continue
(if employment not permanent)

Expiry date
(if employment is for a fixed term)

JOB TITLE
(state title of job employed to do, or give brief description of work for which employed)

Note 2 applies *

REMUNERATION
(state scale or rate of remuneration, or method of calculation, and the intervals at which remuneration is paid)

Note 3a applies *

Note 3b applies *

HOURS OF WORK
(state any terms and conditions relating to hours of work, including any terms and conditions relating to normal hours of work)

Note 4a applies *

Note 4b applies *

Note 4c applies *

HOLIDAYS AND HOLIDAY PAY
(state holidays, including public holidays, and holiday pay. The particulars given must be sufficient to enable entitlement, including any entitlement to accrued holiday pay on the termination of employment, to be precisely calculated)

Note 5a applies *

Note 5b applies *

Note 5c applies *

(If there are no particulars to be entered in this section, enter N/A here)

When any of the above particulars change, the employer will, not later than one month after the change, provide a written statement containing particulars of the change.

Signature for
and on behalf
of EMPLOYER

Date

Signature of
EMPLOYEE

Date

- who will pay them their *wages* or give them their pay slip, where and when
- rules about *company property* and *cash handling*
- customer service and other *key work standards*
- any special *terminology* used.

Even if they have done similar work before, there will be some ways of doing things which are different. Some of these may have come out during the interview. In any case, talk to your recruit to try to establish the differences. That will help you to focus on the key things they will need to learn.

Try to look at things through their eyes. You may not have many of your working routines committed to paper. Now could be the time to try to compile a few simple checklists or flow charts showing what happens to particular inputs to your processes – information, raw material, etc.

You don't have to do it all yourself. In fact the people who are closest to each aspect may find it quite illuminating to try to capture exactly what they do, in what sequence, and what happens in the case of rejects or failures. They may even be able to simplify the process before the new recruit gets there. Even if they can't, it will be a lot less bewildering for the newcomer if someone can explain, step by step, how to approach each task.

Decide who can best act as a 'mentor', to help them settle in. You may want to do it yourself, or delegate it to someone who will be working more closely with the newcomer. Ideally it should be someone who can 'show them the ropes', of both the job and the company, without teaching them bad habits. There's more guidance on how to handle this in *Getting a Result*.

With a little forethought, you can make sure the newcomer quickly becomes an effective member of your team. The one thing that will really upset him or her, though, is any slip-up where their pay is concerned. In the final section of this chapter, we will explore how you can reduce the chances of this.

Setting up the payroll

If you have followed the guidance given earlier in this chapter, you will have decided whether to pay weekly or monthly, in cash or by giro or credit transfer. You will also have decided the amount and basis of payment.

If this recruit is the first person you have actually employed, contact your local Tax Office. Seek their advice and make sure you understand their requirements. Ask for a copy of *The Employer's Guide to PAYE*. Talk through the documentation, and establish whether your tax and National Insurance bill will need to be met monthly or quarterly. (Remember, also, to contact your insurance broker and arrange Employers' Liability cover. A copy of the certificate must be displayed in each workplace. This is mandatory from the moment you employ your first person – whether full time or part time.)

Set up a procedure for calculating how much the employee is entitled to in each payment period. If pay is related to hours worked, you may need a signing-in sheet or other means of checking how many hours have actually been put in. If overtime is paid at premium rates, these hours must be calculated separately. If there is a bonus, establish a formula for calculating what has been earned and a means of checking claims. If, for example, a mechanic gets £1.00 per machine on top of basic pay, you need to record how many machines he or she has fixed this month and hence how much money is due.

If this is their first job, or their earnings will be below the tax threshold, or you are not given a P45, ask your new employee to complete Inland Revenue form P46, and send it to the Tax Office. If they are students in full-time education, working for you in their holidays, complete Form P38(S) and ask the student to sign it. This must be submitted to the Tax Office as part of your year-end return – see below.

For all other new employees you will need to:

- Complete *Certificate P45* – parts 2 and 3. This should have been given to them by their previous employer. Send part 3 to your Tax Office and keep part 2 safely as it contains information about previous pay received and tax paid in the year to date.
- Make sure you know how much *National Insurance* and *Income Tax* to deduct from each payment. The Department of Social Security Contribution Tables will enable you to work out how much National Insurance you and the employee must pay. Current copies of the Inland Revenue's PAYE Tax Tables will help you work out the employee's taxable pay and tax due under Pay As You Earn.
- Avoid making any unauthorised deductions from the employee's pay. Apart from PAYE, National Insurance and payments under a court order, it is illegal to make *any* deductions without the employee's written consent. This applies to all employees.
- Keep proper records. For everyone who earns more than the PAYE threshold, use the official *Deductions Working Sheet* (*Form P12*) to record your employee's name, tax code, pay, earnings on which National Insurance contributions are payable by the employee, the amount of National Insurance and income tax deducted, and any Statutory Sick Pay (SSP) or Statutory Maternity Pay (SMP) due. (You will find more on SSP and SMP in *Keeping the Team in Shape*.) At the end of the tax year you will have to complete an end-of-year tax return (*Form P14/60*) for each employee and a summary for all employees on *Form P35*, so keep cumulative totals as you go along.

  Remember, though, that if you keep employee records on a computer database you will need to contact the Data Protection Registrar (see Useful Addresses) for a licence under the Data Protection Act.
- Calculate how much you owe the employee, how much must

be deducted and therefore how much cash you will need or the amount of the credit transfer to be made. Make the necessary arrangements with the bank.

- Prepare an *itemised pay statement* for each employee before each pay day. This is a legal requirement if you employ 20 or more people on contracts for more than eight hours per week, and is worth doing to get things on a business-like footing and save misunderstandings. It should show:

  employee's name
  date
  period for which payment is made
  National Insurance number (optional)
  tax code (optional)
  bank account number and sort code (for credit transfer)
  basic pay for this pay period, indicating basis of calculation
  allowances and additional payments, with reasons
  total gross pay
  tax deducted
  NI deducted
  pension contribution (if applicable)
  any other *authorised* deductions
  net payment enclosed or at the bank.
- pay in the amounts deducted for National Insurance and tax on the due date and handle other paperwork as instructed by the Inland Revenue. If you are ever in any doubt, contact your local Tax Office for advice.

When you hand over your new employee's first payslip, take a little time to make sure he or she understands it and how the payment has been calculated. At the same time, you can find out how the first week or month has gone, and see if there is anything else you should be planning to help your newest recruit settle and succeed.

Good luck to you both!

Useful Addresses

Advisory Conciliation and Arbitration Service (ACAS)
Regional offices
(Head Office)
27 Wilton Street
London
SW1X 7AZ
Telephone: 071 210 3000

British Insurance Brokers Association
BIBA House
14 Bevis Marks
London
EC3A 7NT
Telephone: 071 623 9043

British Safety Council
70 Chancellors Road
London
W6 9RS
Telephone: 081 741 1231

British Standards Institution
2 Park Street
London
W1A 2BS
Telephone: 071 629 9000

Central Office of Industrial Tribunals
(England and Wales)
Southgate Street
Bury St Edmunds
Suffolk
IP33 2AQ
Telephone: 0284 762300

(Scotland)
St Andrew House
141 West Nile Street
Glasgow
G1 2RU
Telephone: 041 331 1601

Chancellor Forms
Formecon Services Ltd
Gateway
Crewe
CW1 1YN
Telephone: 0270 500800

Commission for Racial Equality
Regional offices
(Head Office)
Elliot House
10–12 Allington Street
London
SW1E 5EH
Telephone: 071 828 7022

Confederation of British Industry (CBI)
Regional offices
(Head Office)
Centre Point
103 New Oxford Street
London
WC1A 1DU
Telephone: 071 379 7400

Data Protection Registrar
Whytecliff House
Water Lane
Wilmslow
Cheshire
SK9 5AX
Telephone: 0625 535711

Department of Employment
Caxton House
Tothill Street
London
SW1H 9HF
Telephone: 071 273 3000

(Scotland)
Chesser House West
502 Gorgie Road
Edinburgh
EH11 3YH
Telephone: 031 443 8731

Department of Social Security Advice Line for Employers
For basic enquiries about:
    National Insurance
    Statutory Sick Pay
    Maternity Pay
Telephone: 0800 393539
(Freephone)

Department of Trade and Industry (DTI)
Regional offices
(Head Office)
Ashdown House
123 Victoria Street
London
SW1E 6RB
Telephone: 071 215 5000

EC Information Office
8 Storey's Gate
London
SW1P 3AT
Telephone: 071 973 1992
Personal callers 10am–1pm
Telephone enquiries 2pm–5pm

Employment Medical Advisory Service
At your local Health and Safety Executive Area Office

Employment Service
St Vincent House
30 Orange Street
London
WC2 7HT
Telephone: 071 839 5600

Equal Opportunities Commission
Regional offices
(Head Office)
Overseas House
Quay Street
Manchester
M3 3HN
Telephone: 061 833 9244

Federation of Small Businesses
Regional offices
(Head Office)
32 Orchard Road
Lytham St Annes
Lancashire
FY8 1NY
Telephone: 0253 720911

Health and Safety Executive
Area offices
(Head Office)
Baynards House
1 Chepstow Place
Westbourne Grove
London
W2 4TF
Telephone: 071 243 6000

Industrial Society
Regional offices
(Information helpline)
48 Bryanstan Square
London
W1H 7LN
Telephone: 071 262 2401

Institute of Directors
116 Pall Mall
London
SW1Y 5ED
Telephone: 071 839 1233

Institute of Personnel and Development
IPD House
Camp Road
London
SW19 4UX
Telephone: 081 946 9100

Insurance Brokers Registration Council
15 St Helens Place
London
EC3A 6DS
Telephone: 071 588 4387

Open College
St Paul's
781 Wilmslow Road
Didsbury
Manchester
M20 2RW
Telephone: 061 434 0007

Open University
Walton Hall
Milton Keynes
MK7 6AA
Telephone: 0908 274066

**Royal Society for the
Prevention of Accidents
(ROSPA)**
Regional offices
(Head Office)
Cannon House
The Priory Queensway
Birmingham
B4 6BS
Telephone: 021 200 2461

Society of Pension Consultants
Ludgate House
Ludgate Circus
London
EC4A 2AB
Telephone: 071 353 1688

The Company Information Service

Your entry to the benefits of IPD membership

As just about every element of personnel and people management becomes more complex and demanding, more and more organisations require professional personnel advice.

By subscribing to the Company Information Service your company will gain access to the most comprehensive personnel management facility in the UK. Your company will have access to our Library Information Services and to our Legal Advisory Unit. You will receive copies of Information Notes and Bibliographies as well as regular issues of *Personnel Management* and *PM Plus*. You will receive Institute membership discounts on a range of books, conferences and courses. In short you will gain entry to the most sophisticated information service available in the field of human resources and one that is normally the exclusive territory of individual members of the Institute of Personnel and Development.

Call 081 946 9100 for further details.